HOTEL

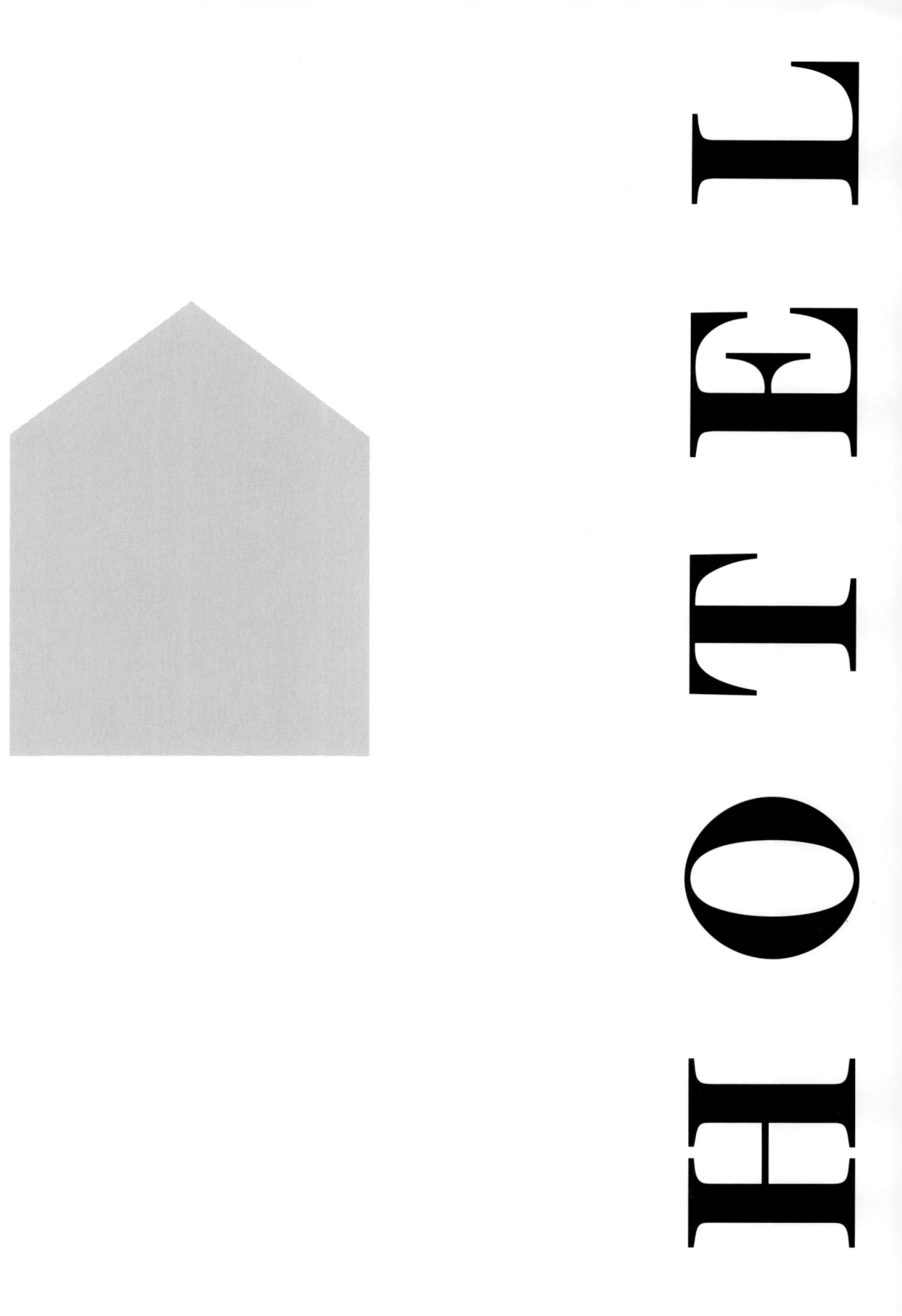

**CHRISTOPH GRÜNIG
SCHWEIZER GASTLICHKEIT
SWISS HOSPITALITY**

CH. GRÜNIG
HOTEL

Schweizer Gastlichkeit
Swiss Hospitality

Texte/Texts

Toni Solidoro

Erwin Stocker

Annelise Leu

Doris Gisler Truog

Christoph Borer

Lian Maria Bauer

ROTHENHÄUSLER VERLAG STÄFA

Impressum

© Rothenhäusler Verlag, CH-8712 Stäfa/Zürich

Herausgeberin/Editor
Barbara Eisl-Rothenhäusler, Zürich

Graphische Gestaltung/Graphic Design
Lilian-Esther Krauthammer, Atelier Perrin, Zürich

Übersetzungen/Translations
Stanley Mason, Effretikon/Zürich

Final Prints
Daniel Aeschlimann, Biel

Fotolithos/Photolithos
Photolitho AG, Gossau/Zürich

Druck und Einband/Printing and Binding
Benziger AG, Einsiedeln

ISBN 3-907960-49-1

VORWORT

Barbara Eisl-Rothenhäusler. Geboren 1956 in Zürich. Gutes Essen und Kochen faszinierten oft mehr als die Schulen. Trotzdem wand sie sich bis zur Matur durch, um anschliessend ihrem Traumberuf an der Hotelfachschule in Lausanne näher zu kommen. Auf die Hotelpraxis folgte die Ausrichtung auf Public Relations und Werbung innerhalb des Tourismus. Seit 1987 ist Barbara Eisl Partnerin in der väterlichen Firma. Die Hobbies Gastronomie und Psychologie mussten seit kurzer Zeit der Liebe zu Gerd und Tochter Fanny weichen.

(M)eine kleine Hotelwelt

Wir sassen nach einem zehnstündigen Fotoarbeitstag im Carnotzet des Hotel Bristol und waren rundum zufrieden. Betreut wurden wir von Frauen und Männern, die uns und die anderen Gäste ganz im Sinne von Marie-Therese Loretan zuvorkommend und liebenswürdig bedienten. Man müsste ein Fotobuch über dieses Bristol machen, meinte Christoph. Wir philosophierten über den unverwechselbaren Geist eines Hotels. Während wir uns den Dôle des Hauses zu Gemüte führten, entstand ein grobes Gerüst für unser Buch. Es sollte ein Buch der vielen gastlichen Häuser in unserem Land sein. Wo Menschen vor und hinter den Kulissen am Werk sind, von denen man leider wenig spricht. Die dazu beitragen, dass unsere Ferien so schön sind; die auch dafür sorgen, dass sich unsere Kinder wohlfühlen; die Freude an ihrem Beruf haben und trotz allen Unkenrufen den Ruhm der Schweizer Hotellerie aufrechterhalten – heute und morgen! Unsere Euphorie hielt auch am Tag darauf an. Wir machten uns an die wohl schwierigste Aufgabe: Die Auswahl der Hotels. Wir fragten möglichst viele Leute nach ihren Lieblingshotels, wir selber hatten auch einige Favoriten. Nach Monaten entstand so etwas wie eine Bestenliste. – Achtzehn Hotels sind in diesem Buch vertreten. Wir meinen, dass es eine Auswahl ist, welche die Schweizer Ferienhotellerie widerspiegelt. Dass vielleicht Ihr Hotel oder Ihr Lieblingshaus nicht dabei ist, bedauern wir. Ohne Zweifel gibt es noch andere Schweizer Hotels, die ebenso sympathisch und einmalig sind. Wir haben eine subjektive Auslese getroffen, die zwischen den beiden roten Buchdeckeln einen angemessenen Platz findet.

Hotels haben auf mich seit jeher eine Faszination ausgeübt. Bereits als neugieriges Kind versuchte ich, die Hotels auch hinter den automatischen Türen zu erkunden. Die Vorliebe für alles Feine aus der Küche weckte zudem den leidenschaftlichen Berufswunsch «Hôtelière». Ich sehnte den ersten Schultag an der berühmten Schule oberhalb Lausanne herbei. Nach vier Jahren anregender Kurse und vielseitiger Hotel-Praktika hielt ich das Diplom in den Händen. Erstens kommt es anders, und zweitens als man denkt: Heute arbeite ich für Hotels, aber nicht in einem Hotel. Die Liebe zu dieser Branche ist geblieben, und es bedeutet für mich eine ganz besondere Freude, dass dieses Buch zustande gekommen ist. Da es mir – bis heute – nicht vergönnt blieb, selber eine Hotelwelt mit ihren Menschen, Zimmern und Räumen, mit Küche und Keller mitzugestalten, ist dieses Buch dank den einfühlenden, teilweise ironischen Fotos von Christoph Grünig vorläufig «mein» kleines, lieb gewonnenes Hotel geworden.

Seit einigen Jahren wird die Schweizer Hotellerie angegriffen. Teilweise zu Recht: Arbeitsbedingungen und das damit verbundene Lamento über Personalmangel und finanzielle Probleme, welche nötige Investitionen oft unmöglich machen, das sind wohl die beiden bösen «Lieblingsthemen» der Branche.

Gestatten Sie mir den Vergleich des Hotels mit einer Familie! Erfahren wir als Gast das Fluidum, die Ambiance als gut und heiter, so stimmt es meistens auch hinter den Kulissen. Wir unterscheiden intuitiv das Künstliche vom Echten. Auch wenn wir nicht sagen können, wo genau es hapert, das ungute Gefühl täuscht uns selten. Wie in der Familie leben die Mitarbeiter in den Ferienhotels während einigen Monaten oder aber das ganze Jahr eng beieinander. Als Gast erleben wir die verschiedenen Bühnenbilder *Hotelzimmer, Frühstücksraum, Empfang, Restaurant, Bar u.s.w.* mit den Schauspielern, die in ihren Berufsrollen stecken.

Bleiben wir beim Frühstück: Fein säuberlich sind die Tische gedeckt, ist das Frühstücksbuffet aufgebaut. Es riecht nach frischen Gipfeli, Zopf, Vollkornbroten. Die geübte Nase wittert den Duft von Kaffee, Rühreiern und gebratenem Speck. Die Früchte, das Birchermüesli, die Milch, die Fruchtsäfte, der Käse und die Konfitüre stehen an ihrem Ort. Die Servicemitarbeiter kommen durch die Schwingtüre, frisch zurechtgemacht, werfen einen prüfenden Blick auf Tische und Stühle, Buffet und Boden – alles ist für den Auftritt der Gäste bereit. Das ältere Ehepaar aus Zimmer 102 ist früh dran, bereit für die Wanderung. Wenig später ertönt das vergnügte Gequietsche des Jüngsten der Familie aus Zimmer 308. Genüsslich machen sich jung und alt am Buffet zu schaffen. Das Buttermödeli wird angeschnitten, das Müesli verliert die liebevoll hingelegte Dekoration aus Nüssen und Dörrfrüchten, die zweite Platte mit frischem Rührei wird ausgewechselt.

Eine kleine Facette aus dem Alltag eines Ferienhotels. Die nachfolgenden Bilder sind amüsante und zum Nachdenken anregende Momentaufnahmen, die Sie mit etwas Fantasie als weitere kleine Bühnenstücke geniessen können. Drei Frauen und drei Männer geben Ihnen mit ihren Texten aus persönlicher Perspektive Einblicke ins Faszinosum Hotel.

FOREWORD

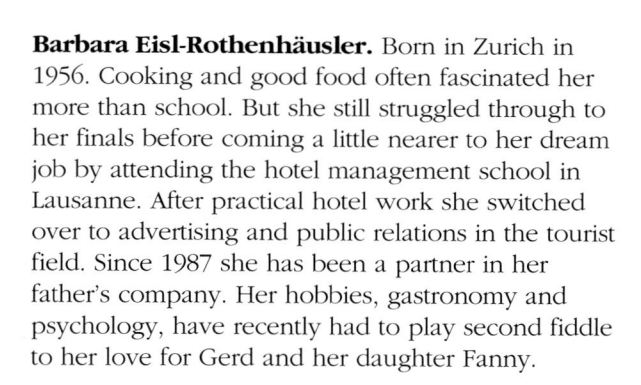

Barbara Eisl-Rothenhäusler. Born in Zurich in 1956. Cooking and good food often fascinated her more than school. But she still struggled through to her finals before coming a little nearer to her dream job by attending the hotel management school in Lausanne. After practical hotel work she switched over to advertising and public relations in the tourist field. Since 1987 she has been a partner in her father's company. Her hobbies, gastronomy and psychology, have recently had to play second fiddle to her love for Gerd and her daughter Fanny.

My Small Hotel World

We were sitting in the rustic wine-sampling carnotzet of the Bristol Hotel after a ten-hour round of photography and were feeling contented with the world. We were being looked after by men and women who attended to our needs and those of the other guests as kindly and obligingly as Marie-Therese Loretan could ever have wished. The Bristol, Christoph mused, ought to be recorded in a book of photographs. We began to philosophize about the inimitable atmosphere of a good hotel. While we sipped the hotel Dôle, a rough plan for our book began to emerge. It was to be a volume on the many hospitable establishments in our country. Where people are at work, on and off the scenes, who get very little publicity. Who do their bit to make our holidays so enjoyable. Who also ensure that our children enjoy themselves. Who like their job and in spite of all carping critics are determined to uphold the fame of Swiss hotels, today and tomorrow. Our euphoria still prevailed on the following day. We made a start on what was no doubt the most difficult task: the choice of hotels. We asked as many people as we could reach about their favourite hotels, and we noted a number of our own. In the course of a few months we thus compiled a list of the best holiday hotels. Eighteen of them are included in this book. We believe it is a selection that mirrors Swiss hoteldom. If your own hotel or favourite home-from-home is not included, we're sorry. We have no doubt that there are a lot of other Swiss hotels that are just as individual and attractive. We have made a subjective choice, just large enough to fit between the two red covers of our book.

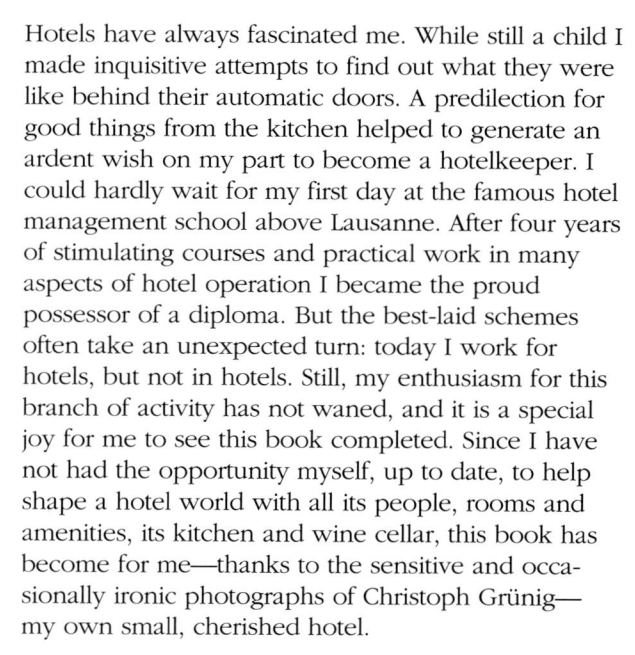

Hotels have always fascinated me. While still a child I made inquisitive attempts to find out what they were like behind their automatic doors. A predilection for good things from the kitchen helped to generate an ardent wish on my part to become a hotelkeeper. I could hardly wait for my first day at the famous hotel management school above Lausanne. After four years of stimulating courses and practical work in many aspects of hotel operation I became the proud possessor of a diploma. But the best-laid schemes often take an unexpected turn: today I work for hotels, but not in hotels. Still, my enthusiasm for this branch of activity has not waned, and it is a special joy for me to see this book completed. Since I have not had the opportunity myself, up to date, to help shape a hotel world with all its people, rooms and amenities, its kitchen and wine cellar, this book has become for me—thanks to the sensitive and occasionally ironic photographs of Christoph Grünig—my own small, cherished hotel.

In the last few years Swiss hotels have come in for a good deal of criticism. Some of it is justified: the working conditions and the lamentable staff shortage and financial problems that often make the necessary investments impossible are today the two most frequently discussed bugbears of the hotel trade. Let me draw a comparison between a hotel and a family. If the guest feels the ambiance to be pleasent and cheerful, things will usually be running smoothly behind the scenes. We have an intuitive feeling for the difference between mere show and genuineness. If we have misgivings in a hotel, we are usually right, even though we cannot say just what is wrong. The staff of resort hotels live in close contact for a few months or a whole year, almost as they would in a big family. The guest then experiences the various settings—*hotel room, breakfast lounge, reception, restaurant, bar* and so forth—complete with the actors who are playing out their professional parts.

To begin with breakfast: The tables are neatly laid, the breakfast buffet carefully arranged. There is a smell of fresh croissants, rolls or wholemeal bread. The gourmet's nose registers the aromas of coffee, scrambled eggs or fried bacon. Fruit, birchermuesli, milk, fruit juices, cheeses and jams form a tempting array. The staff members enter through the swing doors, themselves carefully groomed, and cast a critical eye over tables, chairs, buffet and floor: everything is as it should be, and ready for the guests. The elderly couple from Room 102 are the first to appear, all dressed up for a morning walk. Seconds later the youngest member of the family from Room 308 can be heard squeaking out his high spirits. All gather in Epicurean absorption around the buffet. The slab of butter is sliced, the muesli loses its lovingly composed decoration of nuts and dried fruit, the second platter of fresh scrambled eggs is replaced.

This is just one small scene from the everyday life of a holiday hotel. The pictures that follow are amusing and thought-provoking snapshots which with a dash of imagination you can enjoy as further scenes from the ongoing play of hotel life.

In our texts three women and three men contribute their personal slants on the fascinating theme of the hotel.

Vom Küchenjungen zum Maître d'hôtel

Seit fünfunddreissig Jahren bin ich in meinem Beruf, seit fünfundzwanzig Jahren als Maître d'hôtel im Hotel Bristol in Leukerbad. In dieser Funktion steht man zwischen der Küche, der Réception, den anderen Abteilungen und der eigenen Servicebrigade. Es wird immer schwieriger, sich durchzusetzen, sich Verständnis zu verschaffen – vor allem bei der jungen Generation. Die Frauen und Männer besuchen schnell eine Hotelfachschule und glauben sich nach der Ausbildung bereits als Vollprofi. Der Beruf des Service ist ein weites Feld, das sich nicht auf das Hin- und Wegtragen von Speis und Trank reduziert. Wir sind für den Speisesaal oder das Restaurant verantwortlich. Das heisst nicht nur für die verkauften Gerichte und Weine, sondern auch für die Sauberkeit des Lokals, das Mobiliar, die Tischwäsche, das Silber, das Geschirr, die Blumen usw. So beginnt die Arbeit früh morgens, wenn ein Teil der Servicemitarbeiter das Frühstück vorbereiten. Die Tische sind am Abend vorher bereits gedeckt worden. Nur die Tassen fehlen; diese tragen wir erst zusammen mit Kaffee oder Tee zum Gast. Was gibt es Besseres als ein heisser Frühstückskaffee aus einer heissen Tasse! Vor dem Mittagsservice saugen wir den Boden gründlich, wechseln die Tischtücher aus und beginnen mit dem sorgfältigen Aufdecken. Im Office – unser rückwärtiger Arbeitsraum – putzen wir die Silberplatten, das Besteck, reiben die Gläser sauber, füllen die Ménagen (Salz und Pfeffer) auf, putzen die Brotkörbchen – alle diese Dinge nennen wir Mise-en-place.

Meine Aufgabe ist es, den Mitarbeitern ihre Aufgaben zu verteilen, Arbeitspläne zu schreiben, mit dem Küchenchef die Tagesangebote zu besprechen, die Gäste zu beraten und zu betreuen, den Überblick nie zu verlieren. Trotz meiner 35jährigen Erfahrung lerne ich jeden Tag dazu, denn wir leben in einer Branche mit vielen Veränderungen. Die Küche hat sich verändert so wie unsere Lebensweise.

Als Maître d'hôtel braucht man eine Elefantenhaut: Die Einwände oder manchmal auch Reklamationen kommen von Gästen, vom Patron und von den Mitarbeitern. Missverständnisse entstehen aus Angst oder wegen Sprachproblemen; sie müssen mit Umsicht richtiggestellt werden. Ein wichtiger Punkt ist die Sauberkeit von uns Serviceleuten. Kurze Haare bei den Männern und die korrekte tägliche Rasur sind unerlässlich. Bei den Frauen erwarte ich einen diskreten Duft eines Eau de Cologne – starke Parfums könnten die Gäste stören. Während dem Service widme ich mich den Gästen, beobachte den Saal, damit alles reibungslos abläuft. Wenn ein Lehrling zulange mit einer Dame am Tisch plaudert, fordere ich ihn diskret auf, seiner Arbeit nachzugehen. In einem Ferienhotel gehört das Gespräch mit dem Gast zu unserer Aufgabe, wo kämen wir aber hin, wenn wir mit allen – das können bis zu hundert Gäste sein – nur redeten...

Das ist einer der Punkte, wieso ich meinen Beruf so liebe. Der Kontakt mit den Menschen, den Mitarbeitern, den Lehrlingen, den Gästen, den Patrons.

Geboren bin ich am 29. Februar 1940 im italienischen Ruffano (Provinz Lecce). Mit 17 Jahren ging ich von zu Hause weg in die Schweiz – ohne Ausbildung, aber mit einem Arbeitsvertrag als Küchenjunge im Hôtel des Voyageurs in Lausanne. Nach einem Monat wurde ich ins Office des Tea Rooms versetzt. Bald darauf beorderte mich der Direktor des Hôtel Château d'Ouchy ins Frühstücksoffice, von wo aus wir die vollbeladenen Tablette in die Hotelzimmer brachten. Hier erhielt ich als Servicelehrling meine ersten Trinkgelder. Die Arbeit machte mir Spass und nach sechs Monaten fragte ich, ob ich im Saal servieren könne. Da mein Französisch noch nicht genügend war, wurde ich abends im Dancing als Chasseur eingesetzt. Nachmittags verkaufte ich Pâtisserie auf der Terrasse. Mein Gehalt betrug 160 Franken im Monat. Als ich um etwas mehr Lohn bat, meinte der Direktor, meine Arbeitskraft sei nicht mehr nötig, ich solle mir eine andere Stelle suchen. Für uns Italiener waren es harte Zeiten, wir wurden schlecht behandelt. Ich wechselte verschiedene Male die Arbeit, lernte gleichzeitig Französisch und Spanisch. Man sagte mir, ich sollte Deutsch lernen, so könnte ich mehr Geld verdienen. So stellte mich 1960 das Hotel Elite in Zürich – ohne Vertrag, nur probeweise – als Saalkellner ein. Kurz danach hiess es, man könne mich wegen meinen ungenügenden Deutschkenntnissen nicht gebrauchen. Ich suchte in ganz Zürich nach einer Stelle, vergeblich. Im nahen Deutschland arbeitete ich während drei Monaten in einer Pizzeria. Ich war nicht glücklich und kehrte nach Italien zurück. An der Grenze hielt man mich auf und wollte, dass ich Militärdienst leiste. Doch als Ältester von acht Söhnen wurde ich bald darauf ausgemustert. Ich nahm die Gelegenheit wahr und reiste wieder in die Schweiz – nach Brig. Zufälligerweise traf ich hier einen Freund, der mir riet, nach Leukerbad ins Hotel Maison Blanche zu gehen. Dort würde man Arbeit finden und auch die Entlöhnung sei gut. Dank meinen Sprachkenntnissen stellte man mich sogleich ein. Es gefiel mir sehr gut hier, ich fühlte mich wohl. Nach zwei Jahren wurde ich 2. Maître d'hôtel und blieb weitere drei Jahre. Es zog mich nach England, doch die Familie Loretan, die ich gut kannte, bat mich, ins Hotel Bristol zu kommen. Das Hotel wurde vergrössert, und im Oktober 1967 begann ich, mit Frau Marie-Therese Loretan und nur wenigen Mitarbeitern, die Arbeit. Es war eine grosse Aufgabe, es gab sehr viel zu tun, aber es gefiel mir ausgezeichnet.

Ich fühle mich geborgen wie in einer grossen Familie, in der alles gut funktioniert. Ich werde respektiert. Seit 25 Jahren.

Toni Solidoro

From Kitchen Boy to Maître d'hôtel

I have worked in my profession for thirty-five years, and for the last twenty-five years I have been maître d'hôtel in the Bristol in Leukerbad. In this position one is situated somewhere between kitchen, reception, other departments and one's own service team. It becomes more and more difficult to impose one's will while establishing a degree of mutual understanding, especially with the younger generation. Young men and women today take a brief course in a hotel management school and then see themselves as full-fledged professionals. But hotel service is a wide field that cannot be reduced to carrying food and drink to and from the guests.

We are responsible for the dining room or restaurant. And not only for the meals and wines but for the cleanliness of the premises, the furniture, the table linen, the silver, the tableware, flowers and so forth. Work begins early in the morning when some of the staff prepare breakfast. The tables have been laid on the previous evening. Only the cups are missing: these will appear only when coffee or tea is served in them. There is nothing better than a hot breakfast coffee from a hot cup! Before lunch we vacuum-clean the floor thoroughly, change the tablecloths and begin carefully laying the tables. In the pantry, our rear workroom, we polish the silver trays, cutlery and glasses, fill the cruets (salt and pepper), clean the bread baskets—tasks which, taken together, we know as *mise-en-place*.

My function is to allocate jobs to the staff, to write out work plans, to discuss the daily supplies with the chef, to advise the guests and attend to their needs, and never to lose track of the general situation. In spite of my thirty-five years of experience, I am learning all the time, for we work in a branch that is constantly changing. The kitchen has changed parallel to our own way of life. A maître d'hôtel needs a thick skin; objections and complaints may come from guests, from his employer or from staff.

Misunderstandings may be caused by apprehension or by language problems, and they must be handled with circumspection. One important point is hygiene on the part of the staff. The men must have their hair cut short and must always be well shaven. I expect the ladies to wear a discreet eau de Cologne—more obtrusive perfumes might disturb the guests. During service I devote myself to the guests, observing the dining room and seeing that everything runs smoothly. If an apprentice talks to a lady guest too long at her table, I discreetly intimate to him that he should get on with his work. In a resort hotel talking with guests is part of our job, but it would never do for us to spend our time chatting with them all—there may well be a hundred of them! But that is one reason why I am so fond of my work; the contacts it brings with people, with staff and apprentices, with guests and employers.

I was born on 29 February 1940 in Ruffano in the province of Lecce, Italy. At seventeen I left home for Switzerland, without any training but with a contract as kitchen boy in the Hôtel des Voyageurs in Lausanne. After a month's work I was moved into the pantry of the tea room. Soon afterwards the director of the Hôtel Château d'Ouchy transferred me to the breakfast pantry, whence we carried the loaded trays into the hotel rooms. Here, as a service apprentice, I got my first tips. I enjoyed the work, and six months later I asked whether I could serve in the dining room. But my French was not yet good enough, and instead I was made a *chasseur* in the dance bar. In the afternoons I sold pastries on the terrace. I was then earning 160 francs a month. When I asked for a rise, the director told me I was no longer needed, I could look for another job. Those were hard times for us Italians, we were badly treated. I changed my job several times, while learning French and Spanish. People told me I ought to learn German, I could then earn a better wage. In 1960 the Hotel Elite in Zurich offered me a post as a waiter, without any contract, just on probation. But shortly afterwards they told me they could no longer make use of my services because my German was not good enough. I looked for work all over Zurich, but in vain. Then I worked in a pizzeria for three months just over the frontier in Germany. But I was unhappy there and returned to Italy. I was held up at the frontier; they wanted me to do military service. But being the eldest of eight sons, I was soon exempted. I made use of my new-gained freedom to go back to Switzerland—this time to Brig. Here I chanced to meet a friend who advised me to try the Maison Blanche hotel in Leukerbad. You could get work there, he said, and the pay was good. On the strength of my knowledge of languages, I was taken on at once. I very much liked the job and felt at home. Two years later I was made deputy maître d'hôtel and stayed on for another three years. I was keen to go to England, but the Loretan family, whom I knew well, asked me to come to the Bristol. The hotel was enlarged, and in October 1967 I started my work there with Marie-Therese Loretan and a small staff. It was a demanding task and there was a great deal to be done, but it pleased me mightily.

I feel at home here, as though I were part of a big family in which everything runs smoothly. I feel respected. And have now been here for twenty-five years.

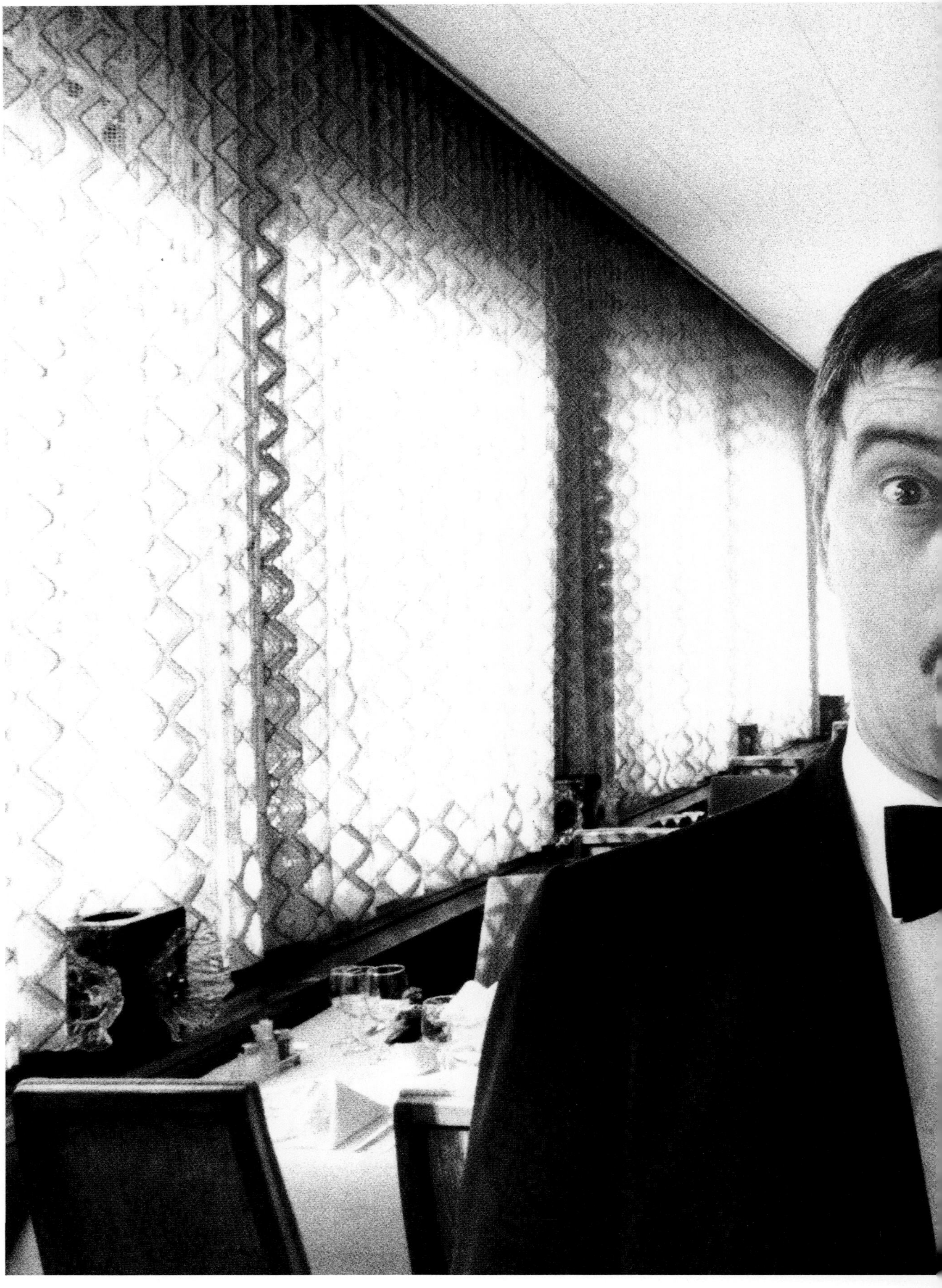

Hotel Bristol, Leukerbad

Märchenhotel Bellevue, Braunwald

Grand Hotel Victoria-Jungfrau, Interlaken

Grand Hôtel des Bains, Yverdon-les-Bains

Hotel Rebstock, Luzern

Gasthof Hirschen am See, Meilen

18

Gasthof Hirschen am See, Meilen

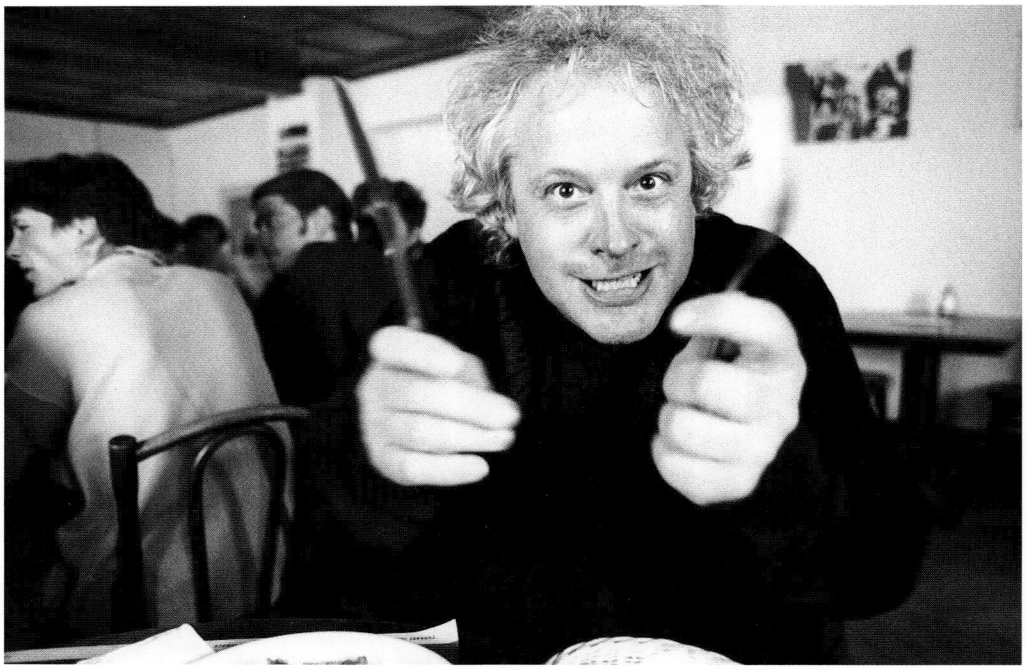

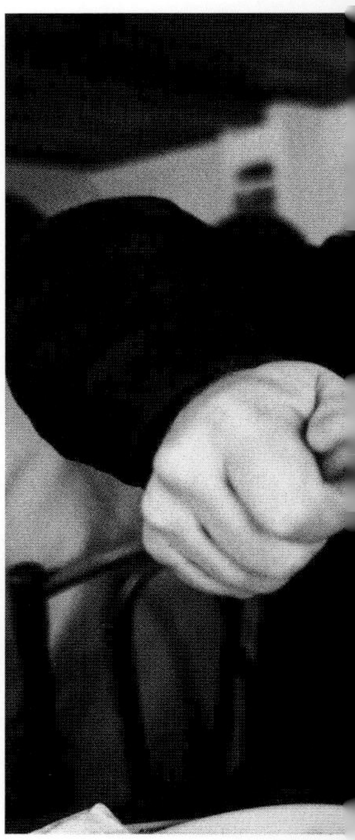

Hotel Furkablick, Realp

22

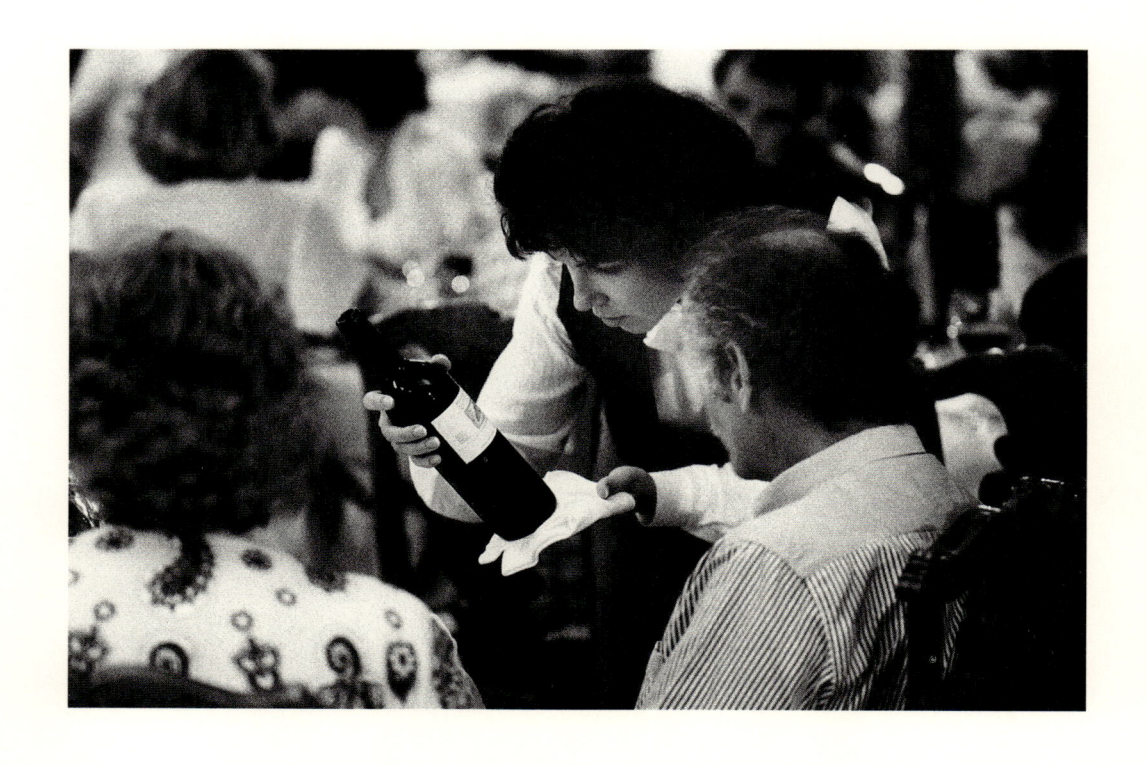

Relais & Châteaux Hôtel Giardino, Ascona

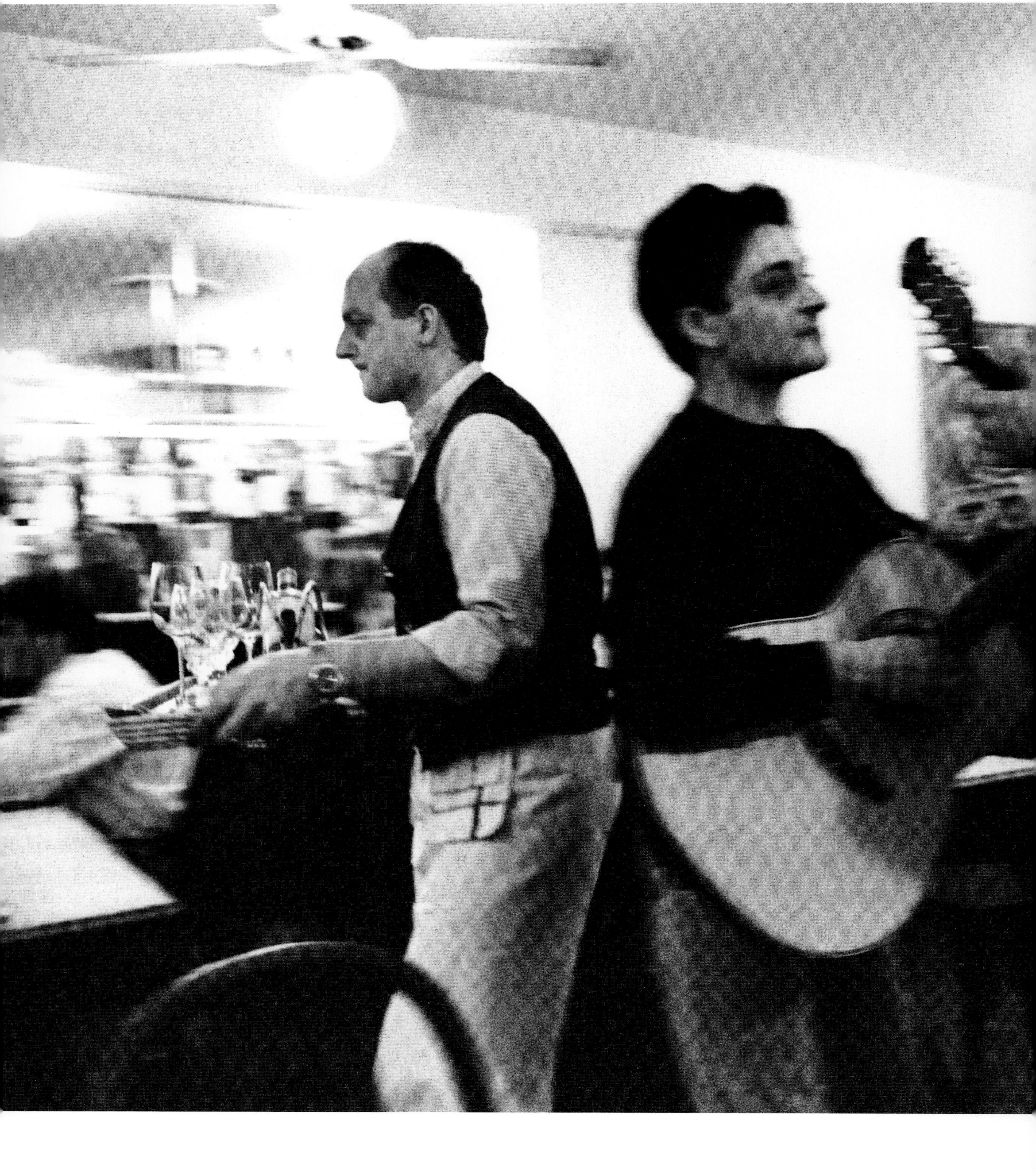

Hotel Rebstock, Luzern

Hotel Europe, Davos

Hôtel Le Vieux Manoir au Lac, Murten

Grand Hotel Victoria-Jungfrau, Interlaken

Der Berufsweg eines Kochs

Im Oberwallis, wo ich aufgewachsen bin, ging man acht Monate ununterbrochen zur Schule, hatte dafür aber vier Monate Sommerferien. Diese nutzte ich, um bei meiner Tante in Zermatt in der Hotelküche mitzuarbeiten. Die Atmosphäre hat mir unauslöschliche Eindrücke hinterlassen. Je lauter es «kesselte», desto besser gefiel es mir. Kinderarbeit? Mitnichten! Die Tätigkeit bereitete mir Freude und ersparte mir den Weg zum Berufsberater, weil ich schon damals wusste, dass ich dereinst Koch werden möchte. Im Herbst 1952 begann ich als 15jähriger in Davos die Lehre. Dabei kam mir die Zeit in Zermatt, in der ich dem Chef hatte helfen dürfen, sehr zugute. Ich war der erste Lehrling im Betrieb, der statt Lehrgeld zahlen zu müssen, zwanzig Franken Monatslohn erhielt. Mein Lehrmeister, Herr Baumgartner, den ich sehr schätzte, war zwar äusserst streng, doch immer korrekt. Er hat mir viel fürs Leben mitgegeben. Auch die Fachlehrer waren hervorragend. Ich erinnere mich gerne an sie, vermittelten sie doch nicht nur Fachwissen, sondern auch Lebensstil- und -Haltung. Die Lehre dauerte damals zweieinhalb Jahre. Mein Berufsschulheft umfasste sage und schreibe 43 Doppelseiten; heutzutage treten die Lehrlinge mit mindestens sechs Bundesordnern zur Abschlussprüfung an. Persönlich meine ich, weniger wäre hier mehr! Lehrer und Lehrlinge gerieten weniger unter Druck und hätten dafür mehr Zeit, sich praktischen Dingen zuzuwenden.

1955 schloss ich mit Erfolg die Lehrzeit ab. Es folgten die Wanderjahre. Mit Recht heisst es, Köche und Zigeuner seien beide fahrendes Volk.

Meine Commis-Zeit war, muss ich gestehen, eine harte Zeit. Trotz der vielen Arbeitsstunden verdiente man wenig; in der dritten Saison im selben Haus wurde mein Gehalt von anfänglichen 170 Franken auf 220 aufgebessert. Im Herbst suchte ich über den Verband Union Helvetia eine Commis-Stelle. So unglaublich es heute tönt, ich fand in der ganzen Schweiz keine! Deshalb nahm ich für die nächsten drei Zwischensaisons eine Stelle an bei einem Metzger in Visp. Der Tätigkeit in der Metzgerei und im Schlachthaus verdanke ich meine Kenntnisse, was Fleisch und dessen Verarbeitung anbetrifft. Wegweisend wurde für mich 1963 die Stelle im Hotel Baur au Lac in Zürich. Dort stimmte nämlich von der Arbeitszeit bis zum Zimmer mit eigenem Lavabo und Kleiderschrank alles. An Herrn Garcin, den damaligen Chef, Verantwortlicher einer 40-Mann-Brigade, habe ich die besten Erinnerungen. Damals spielte ich öfters mit dem Gedanken, selbst einmal einer grossen Brigade vorzustehen. Im Herbst 1969 fuhr ich mit der New Amsterdam, dem Flaggschiff der Holland Amerika-Lijn, für zwei Monate in die Karibik. Im Dezember gleichen Jahres trat ich meine erste Stelle als Chef Tournant, später als Chef Saucier im Park Lane Hotel in London an. Auch diese Anstellung hinterliess mir nachhaltige Eindrücke: Die Brigade zählte 120 Mann. Die Eröffnung mit ersten Banketten, tausend geladenen Gästen und einem Menu von sechs Gängen dauerte drei Tage. Die Grossküchen-Atmosphäre auf hohem Niveau bleibt mir unvergesslich. 1971 wurde ich Küchenchef im neuen Hotel Metropole in Interlaken, wo ich während zehn Jahren tätig war. Es war eine äusserst berufsintensive Zeit, war ich doch gleichzeitig Fachlehrer an der Schule, Prüfungs-Obmann und beteiligte mich an Kochkunst-Ausstellungen, wo ich persönlich oder als Mitglied einer Mannschaft zahlreiche erste Preise holte. 1982 verliess ich Interlaken mit einem tränenden Auge. Als neue Herausforderung stand mir die Eröffnung des Hyatt Hotels in Montreux bevor. Dank dessen, dass das Hotel nicht termingerecht abgegeben wurde, kam ich in den Genuss, der Einweihung des Hyatt Hotels in Kuwait beizuwohnen.

Doch wie so oft im Leben kommt es anders, als man denkt: Seit 1984 bin ich im «Victoria-Jungfrau» in Interlaken und stehe einer 40 bis 50 Mann grossen Brigade vor. Mein Lebensziel habe ich erreicht! Wenn ich zurückblicke, hat sich vieles verändert. Während es unser Traum war, einmal in einem grossen Haus Chef einer grossen Mannschaft zu werden, ist für die heutige Generation die Küche zur Durchgangsstation geworden. Worauf man Wert legt, ist, sagen zu können: «Ich habe auch einmal in der Küche gearbeitet; ich kenne die Anforderungen und die entsprechenden Probleme einer Hotelküche.» Ebenso hat sich das Bild des Chefs geändert. Denke ich an meine Lehrlings- und Wanderjahre zurück, ging bei den Vertretern der alten Garde, für die ich nach wie vor viel Respekt empfinde, parallel zum Austausch von privater und Berufskleidung jeweilen ein Wechsel des Verhaltens einher: In Berufskleidung kamen sie mir manchmal wie «Satane» vor, die sozusagen bei jeder Gelegenheit an der Decke «hingen». In Zivil waren sie jedoch wie gute Väter, die ihren Schützlingen manchen guten Rat fürs Leben mitgegeben haben. Mein Anliegen ist es ebenfalls, junge, flotte Leute aufzubauen. Was mich besonders freut, ist, dass sich wieder Lehrlinge melden, die idealistisch eingestellt sind und sich für den Beruf und die Gastronomie engagieren wollen. Denn – was wäre echte Gastfreundschaft ohne den Idealismus der «Gastgeber»?

Erwin Stocker

A Cook's Progress

In the Upper Valais, where I grew up, we went to school for eight months without a break, but had four months of summer holidays. I used this time to work in my aunt's hotel kitchen in Zermatt. The atmosphere of the place left indelible impressions. The louder the noise of the pots and pans, the better I liked it. Child labour? Not a bit af it! I enjoyed the work, and it saved me going to a vocational guidance centre, since I already knew that I wanted to be a cook. In the autumn of 1952, when I was fifteen, I started my apprenticeship in Davos. The time I had spent helping the head cook in Zermatt now came in very useful. I was the first apprentice in the establishment who got a monthly wage of twenty francs instead of having to pay for tuition. My instructor, a Herr Baumgartner, whom I very much liked, was extremely strict but always correct. He taught me a lot that was to stand me in good stead in my later life. The teachers of special subjects were also excellent. I think back to them with pleasure, for they passed on knowledge not only about their own subject but about lifestyles and deportment in general. An apprenticeship at that time lasted two-and-a-half years. My exercise book consisted of just 43 double pages. Today apprentices face their final examination with at least six thick files. Personally, I think less would be more. Instructors and apprentices would then suffer less stress and would have more time for practical matters. I completed my apprenticeship successfully in 1955. The years as a journeyman followed. There's some truth in the saying that cooks and gypsies are wayfaring folk.

My travelling years were, I must admit, hard going. We earned very little in spite of the long hours. In my third season in the same house my wages were raised from 170 to 220 francs a month. In the autumn I tried to get a new job through the Union Helvetia. Incredible as it must sound today, I couldn't find one anywhere in Switzerland. So for the next three intermediate seasons I took a job with a butcher in Visp. I owe my knowledge of meat and how to handle it to my work in the butcher's shop and the abattoir. My future was decided by a post I got in the Hotel Baur au Lac in Zurich in 1963. There everything was just right, from the working hours to a room with a wash-basin and wardrobe. Herr Garcin, then chef and head of a brigade of forty, made a very favourable impression on me. At that time I often imagined being in charge of a big team myself. In autumn 1969 I travelled to the Caribbean for two months on the New Amsterdam, the flagship of the Holland-America Line. In December of the same year I took up my first post as Chef Tournant, later Chef Saucier, in Park Lane Hotel, London. This job also left a deep impression: the brigade comprised 120 persons. The opening with the first banquets, a thousand guests and a six-course menu lasted three days, and I shall never forget the atmosphere of the big kitchen working to the highest standards. In 1971 I became chef in the new Hotel Metropole in Interlaken, where I stayed for ten years. It was a very busy time, for I was also teaching at the catering school there, was head of the examining committee and was taking part in cookery exhibitions, where I won numerous first prizes either on my own account or as a member of a team. In 1982 I left Interlaken, not without regrets. I had a new challenge to face in the form of the Hyatt Hotel that was opening in Montreux. As the Hotel was not ready in time, I was able before commencing work to be present at the opening of the Hyatt Hotel in Kuwait. Yet as so often in life, things took a turn I had not expected. Since 1984 I have headed a team of 40–50 persons in the Victoria-Jungfrau Hotel in Interlaken. I have now attained the goal I originally set myself.

A backward glance shows that there have been great changes since my youth. While we used to dream of being in charge of a large team in a leading hotel, the new generation often regards the kitchen only as one station on their way. They like to be able to say: "I once worked in the kitchen too; I know the requirements and the problems of hotel kitchens." The conception of the chef de cuisine has also changed. Back in the days when I was an apprentice and a journeyman, the members of the old guard—for whom I still have a good deal of respect—used to change their behaviour whenever they changed from professional to civil togs; dressed as cooks, they often seemed to me satanic and would explode with rage at every opportunity, whereas in civil garb they were kindly father figures who often gave their wards useful advice. It is also my objective to train lively and able young people. It is a particular pleasure to me that there are again more apprentices with an idealistic outlook, who are really dedicated to their profession and to gastronomy in general. For what would hospitality be without a fund of idealism on the part of the host?

Hôtel de la Gare, Le Noirmont

Relais & Châteaux Hôtel Giardino, Ascona

Hotel Hirschen, Meilen

Hotel Bristol, Leukerbad

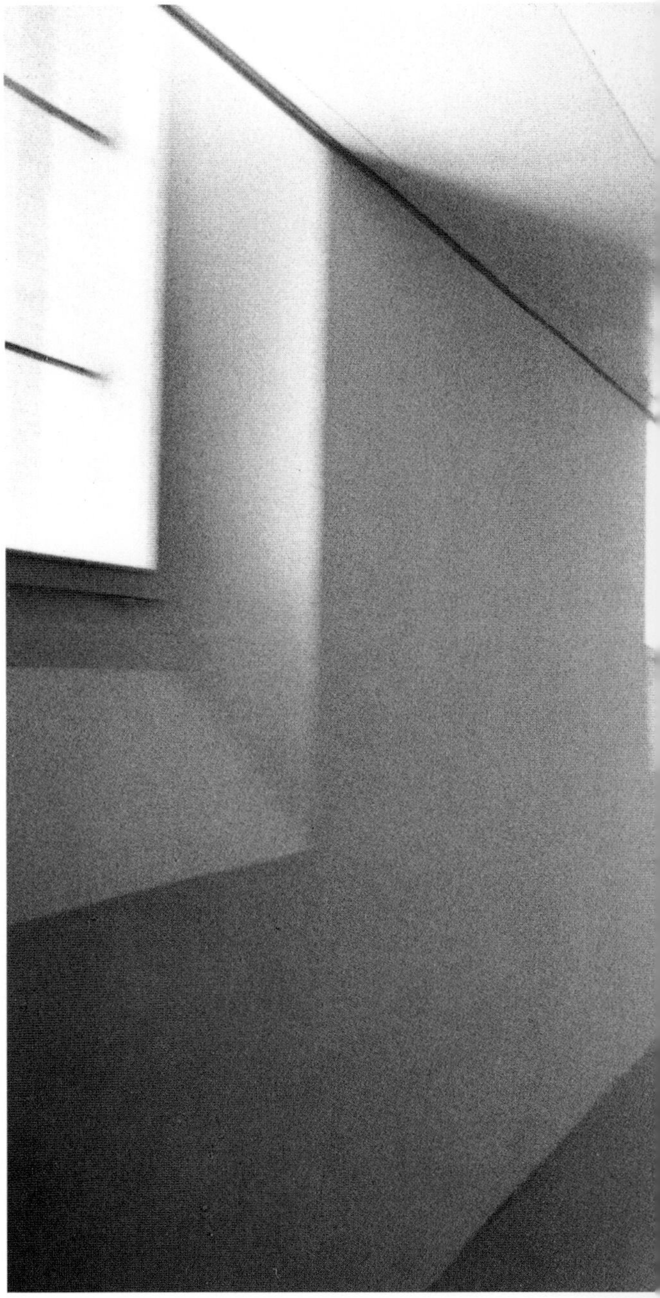

Grand Hotel Victoria-Jungfrau, Interlaken

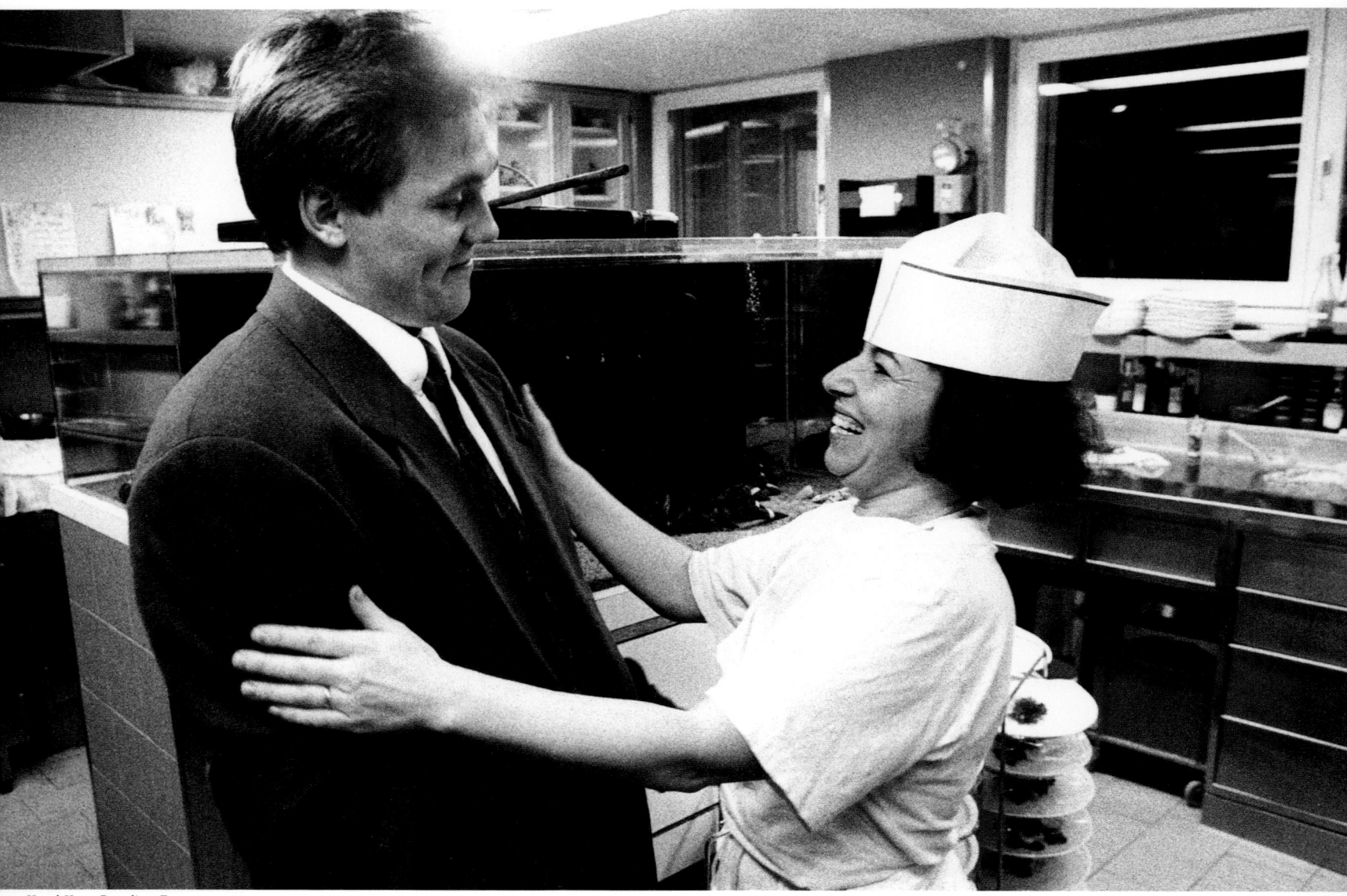

Hotel Haus Paradies, Ftan

Hotel Bristol, Leukerbad

Annelise Leu. Geboren 1931 in Basel. Den Traum des Musikstudiums redete ihr ihr Vater aus mit dem Hinweis, Annelise sollte nicht von ihrem «Stimmeli» leben müssen. So entschied sie sich für die Hotellerie, die sie an der Lausanner Hotelfachschule kennen- und schätzen gelernt hat. Zusammen mit ihrem Mann Hans C. Leu arbeitete sie an verschiedenen Saisonstellen, bevor sie ihre drei Kinder Livia, Martina und Christian aufzog. Von 1966 bis 1986 arbeitete sie als Direktorin im Kulm Hotel Arosa. 1974 entschloss sie sich zum Kauf des Hôtel le Vieux Manoir au Lac am Murtensee – das Risiko voll abschätzend. 1984 übernahm sie die Aktienmehrheit des Hotel Eden Arosa, in dem sie sich als Delegierte des Verwaltungsrates engagiert. Als Unternehmerin und Hôtelière kämpfte sie sich zum Erfolg durch und kennt auch die rauhen Seiten dieser Branche. Der Musik ist Annelise Leu treu geblieben – Gesang und Klavier sind ihre zweite Leidenschaft.

Das Hotel – ein Mikrokosmos

Ein Hotel ist eine kleine, faszinierende Welt für sich – künstlich gestaltet von Menschenhand, nach aussen abgegrenzt durch eine glänzende Fassade, dazu geschaffen, eine ausgewählte Schar von Menschen speziell zu verwöhnen. Hotels können in ihrem Angebot auch einfach sein und zu günstigen Preisen den Ansprüchen einer Kundschaft mit bescheidenerem Budget gerecht werden. Ebenso kann sich ein Hotel auf eine bestimmte Gruppe von Leuten ausrichten, zum Beispiel auf Geschäftsleute in einer Stadt, auf Sportler in den Bergen oder auf Senioren in einem Wohnheim. So vielfältig wie das Leben präsentieren sich die verschiedenen Hotels.

Für mich soll ein Hotel ein Ferien-Paradies sein für eine buntgemischte Gästeschaft, wo fröhliche Menschen Vergnügen finden; eine Bühne für die grosse Schau, bei der man selbst mitspielen kann. Elegante Gäste gehen durch das Frontportal ein und aus, geniessen ein feines Essen im Schlemmer-Restaurant, amüsieren sich an der Bar und sind sich meist wohl kaum bewusst, dass sie nur die eine Seite, die Sonnenseite der Mini-Weltkugel wahrnehmen; dass hinter den Kulissen, auf der Rückseite des Hauses, eine andere Seite des Lebens stattfindet, die ergänzende Hälfte, die die Kugel erst rund und voll macht.

Eine gigantische geheimnisvolle Maschinerie hält die Hotel-Welt in Schwung, angetrieben von Menschen, die zur Hintertüre hineingehen, wo sich in Küchen, Kellern und Abwaschräumen ein ebenso intensives Leben abspielt. Hinten wie vorne wird gelacht; doch während der Gast beim Tanz und vom Genuss köstlichen Weins ins Schwitzen gerät oder sich in der Sauna künstlich aufheizen lässt, verdient der Koch im Schweisse seines Angesichts sein tägliches Brot am heissen Herd.

Auf der Nahtstelle, dort wo die zwei Hälften ineinandergreifen, steht der Hotelier. Er verbindet die beiden Welten, geht hin und her, lebt sowohl mit den Gästen als auch mit seinen Mitarbeitern. Selbst eine Frau kann Hôtelière sein, wie in meinem Fall; meist aber sind sie zu zweit, Mann und Frau, damit die Welt komplett ist.

Wir haben den schönsten Beruf, den es gibt. Ein Hotel ist zwar eine künstliche Welt, aber sie muss geschaffen werden, und in meinem Hotel bin ich der Schöpfer. Oder der Kapellmeister, der die verschiedenen Stimmen gemäss der Partitur einübt und zum harmonischen Zusammenklang führt, oder sogar der Komponist, der die Partitur selbst schreibt und alsdann das Werk zur Aufführung bringt. Vielleicht sogar der Verleger und Herausgeber, der zusätzlich für die Finanzen verantwortlich ist.

«L'Hôtelier, c'est un métier complet», haben wir an der Hotelfachschule gelernt. An nahezu allen Berufen hat der Hotelier ein Stück weit Anteil. Meinen Beruf sehe ich als ein lebendes Gesamt-Kunstwerk, das ich gestalten kann. Ich darf mit meinen Gästen zu Tische sitzen und die Früchte geniessen, die wir hervorbringen. Allerdings ist mein Herz noch mehr auf der Hinterseite unserer Mini-Weltkugel, bei den Menschen, die uns in grosser, gemeinsamer Anstrengung das kleine Kunstwerk erschaffen. Ihnen gebührte mehr Anerkennung und Wertschätzung. Denn sie leben in dieser Welt, in der der Gast nur zu Besuch ist; sie sind gleichzeitig Teil und Erzeuger derselben.

Ich freue mich über dieses Buch. Es zeigt in herrlichen Bildern das Hotelleben von allen Seiten, die ganze, volle, runde Kugel, die Welt, in der und für die ich lebe und die zu erschaffen und zu gestalten eine ungeheuer spannende und faszinierende Aufgabe ist.

Annelise Leu

Annelise Leu. Born in Basle in 1931. Her father talked her out of her dream of studying music by saying that she ought not to have to live on her voice. So she opted for the hotel trade, which she got to know and appreciate at the hotel management school in Lausanne. She worked in various seasonal posts with her husband, Hans C. Leu, before bringing up her three children Livia, Martina and Christian. From 1966 to 1986 she worked as directrice in the Kulm Hotel, Arosa. In 1974 she decided to buy the Hôtel le Vieux Manoir au Lac on the Lake of Morat, though fully aware of the risk involved. In 1984 she took over a controlling interest in the Eden Hotel, Arosa, where she became Managing Director. She had to fight her way to success as an entrepreneuse and hôtelière and consequently knows the seamier sides of the branch. She has remained true to her music—singing and piano-playing are still her second passion.

The Hotel—a Microcosm

A hotel is a small but fascinating world of its own—designed by human beings, bounded on the outside by a handsome façade, conceived to pamper a select group of people. Hotels can of course be simple, with moderate prices adapted to the needs of guests with a modest budget. Or a hotel may be aimed at a definite class of people, for instance those who come to a city on business, sportsmen staying in the mountains or elderly people requiring the ambiance of a home. In fact, hotels are as diverse as life itself.

To my mind a hotel ought to be a holiday paradise for a mixed clientele, a place where cheerful people enjoy staying; and a stage for a show in which everyone can play his part. Well-dressed guests enter and leave at the front door, linger over a delicious meal in the gourmet restaurant, amuse themselves at the bar and for the most part are hardly aware that they see only the sunny side of this mini-world, while behind the scenes, at the back of the house, another side of life is enacted, the complementary half that makes this small globe a world in little.

A huge but secret machinery keeps the hotel world functioning; it is driven by people who enter and leave at the back door, where a no less intense life goes on in the kitchens, cellars and washrooms. People laugh in both halves of the hotel, but while the guests will only glow when they dance, after a glass or two of excellent wine, or in the sauna that they enter of their own free will, the cooks must earn their daily bread by the sweat of their brow in the hot kitchen.

At the interface where the two halves mesh stands the hotelier. He connects the two worlds, moves from one to the other, lives with the guests no less than with his working colleagues. The hotelier may of course be a woman, as in my own case, and in the majority of establishments there are in fact two of them, man and wife, so that the world is completed.

We have the finest of all professions. A hotel is an artificial world, but it has to be created, and in my hotel I am the creator. A sort of conductor, who practises with the various instruments that figure in the score and brings them into harmonious accord, if not even the composer, who must first write the score before supervising its performance. And in a way the publisher too, who is responsible for financial control.

"L'hôtelier, c'est un métier complet," we learnt at the hotel management school. In fact, the hotelier combines a little bit of all the professions. I see my job as a living *gesamtkunstwerk*, a synthesis of the arts, and one that I can shape myself. I can even sit at table with my guests and enjoy the fruits of our labours. My heart, however, is more on the other side of our mini-world, with the people who turn out the little work of art in a big joint effort. They deserve more recognition and appreciation. For they really live in this world, which the guest is only visiting; they are its generators, as well as being part of it.

This book fills me with pleasure. Its splendid pictures show hotel life from all angles, the whole, round globe I live in and live for, and the creation and shaping of which is such an exciting and fascinating task.

Park Hotels Waldhaus, Flims

Grand Hotel Victoria-Jungfrau, Interlaken

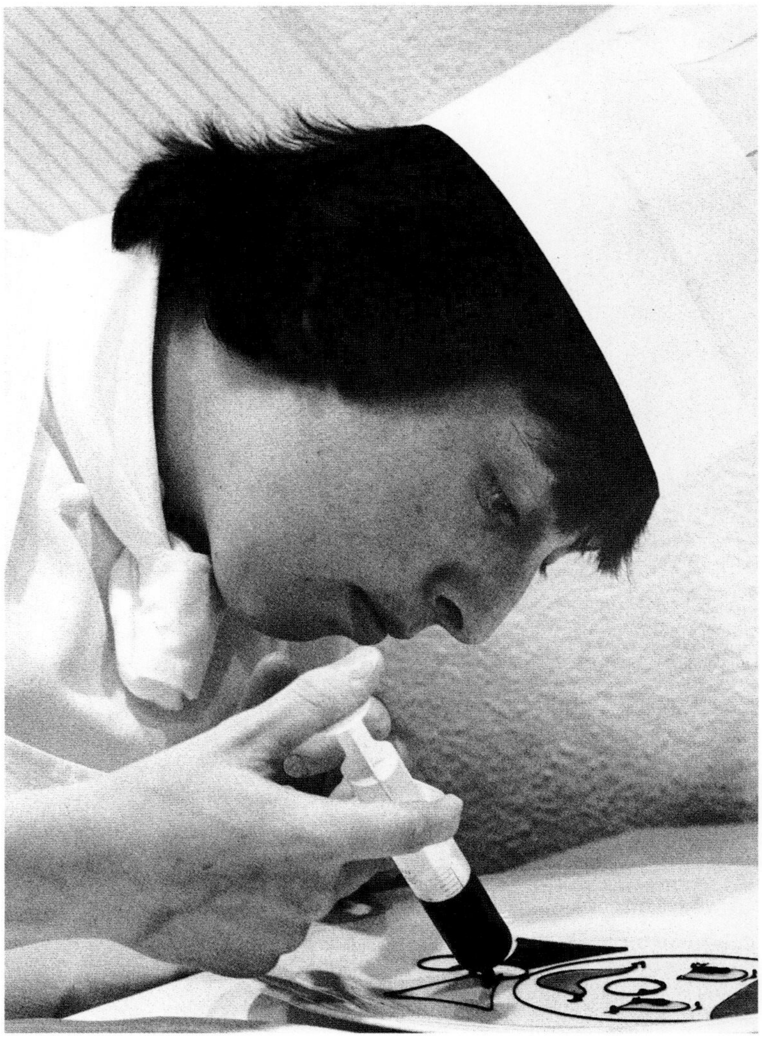

Hotel Haus Paradies, Ftan

Park Hotels Waldhaus, Fl

Hotel Bristol, Leukerbad

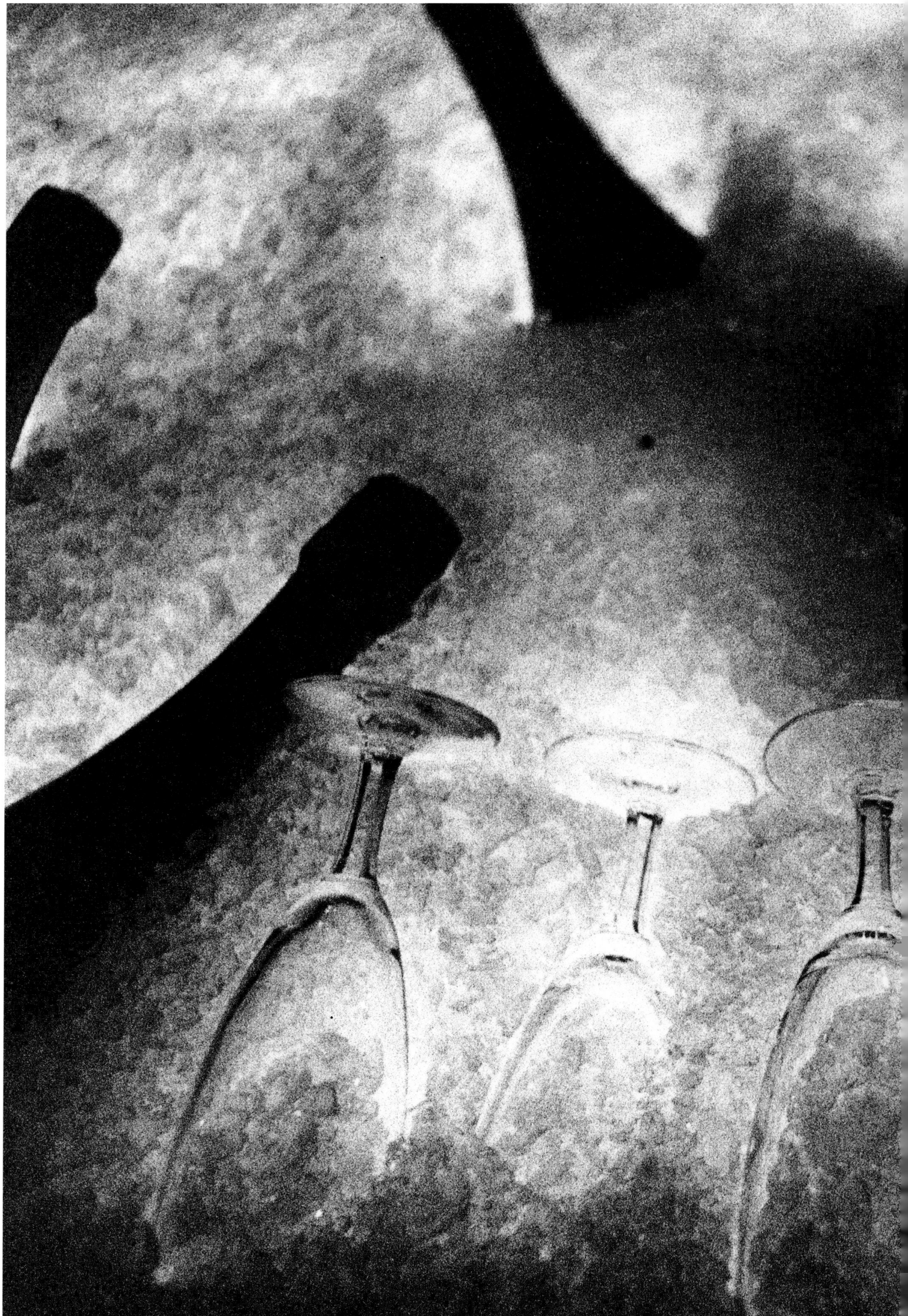

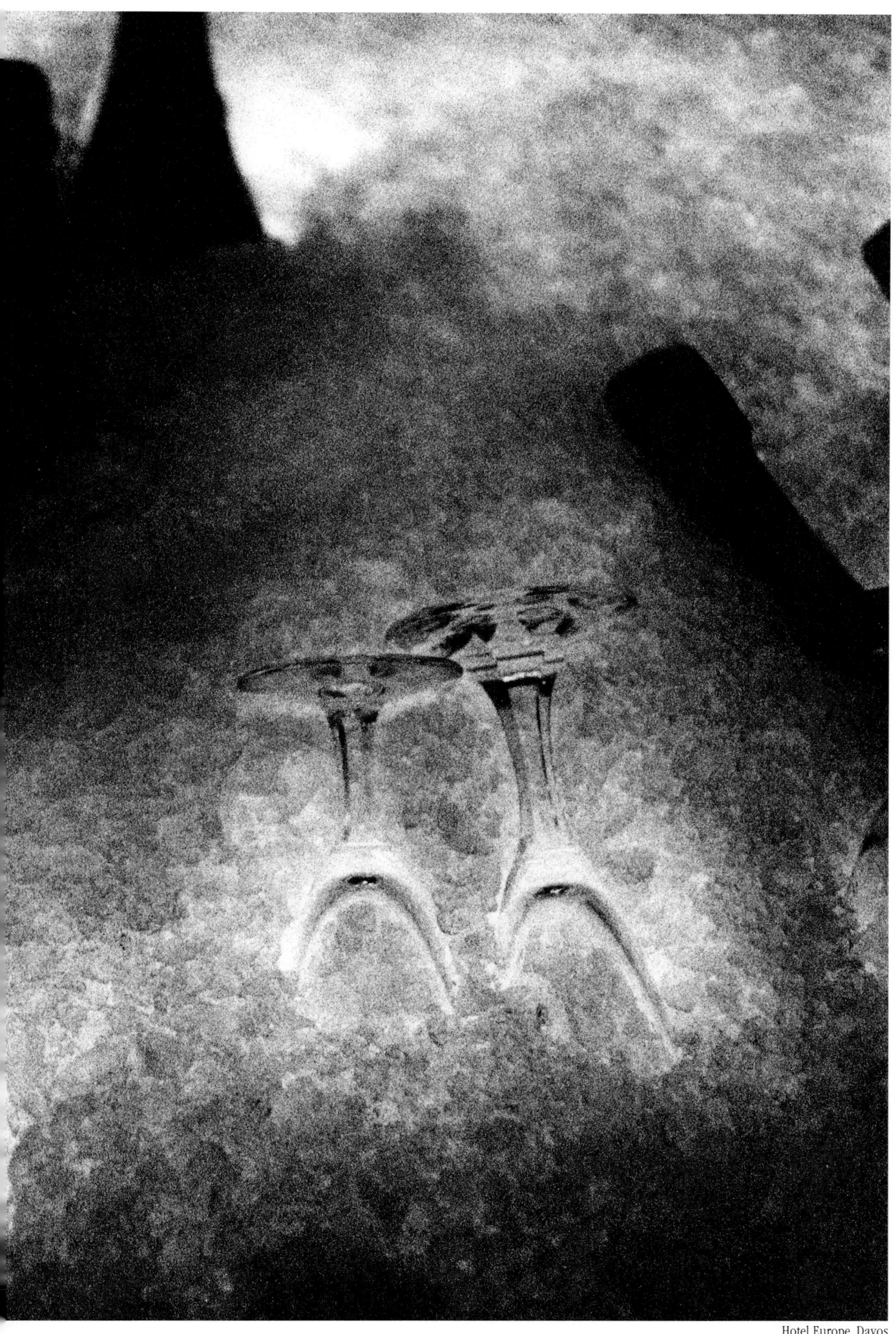

Hotel Europe, Davos

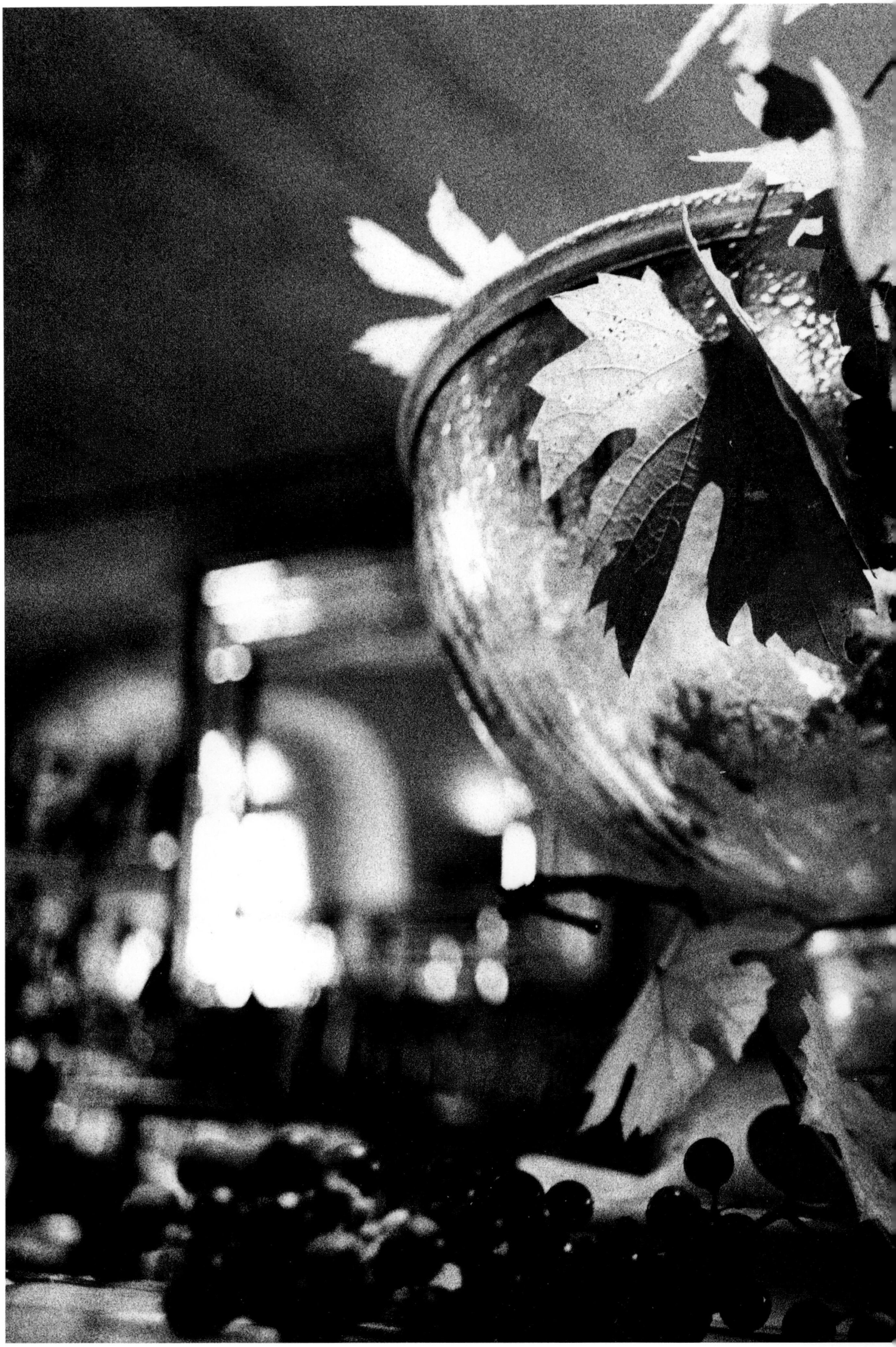

Gasthof Hirschen am See, Meilen

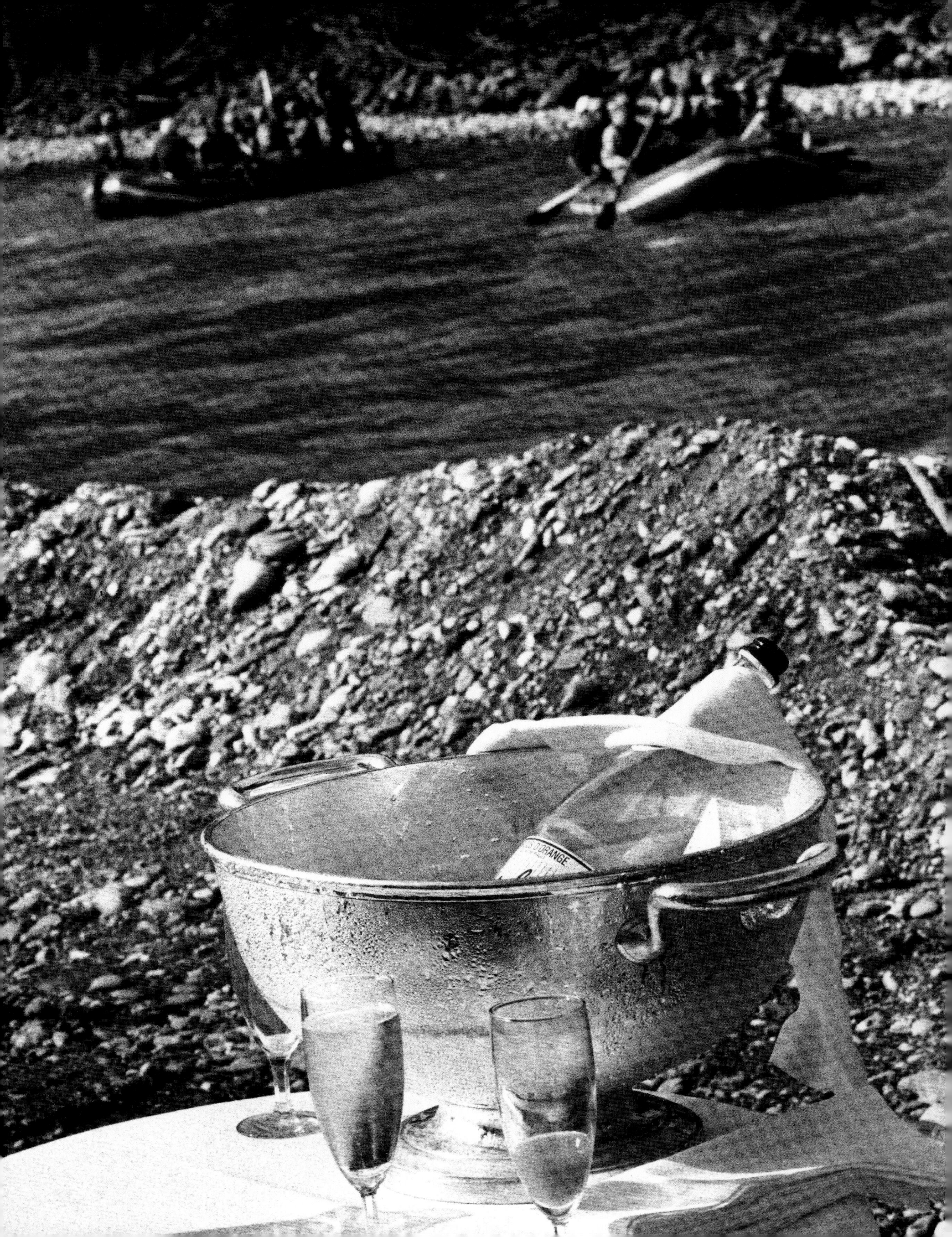
D'ORANGE

Hotel Bristol, Leukerbad

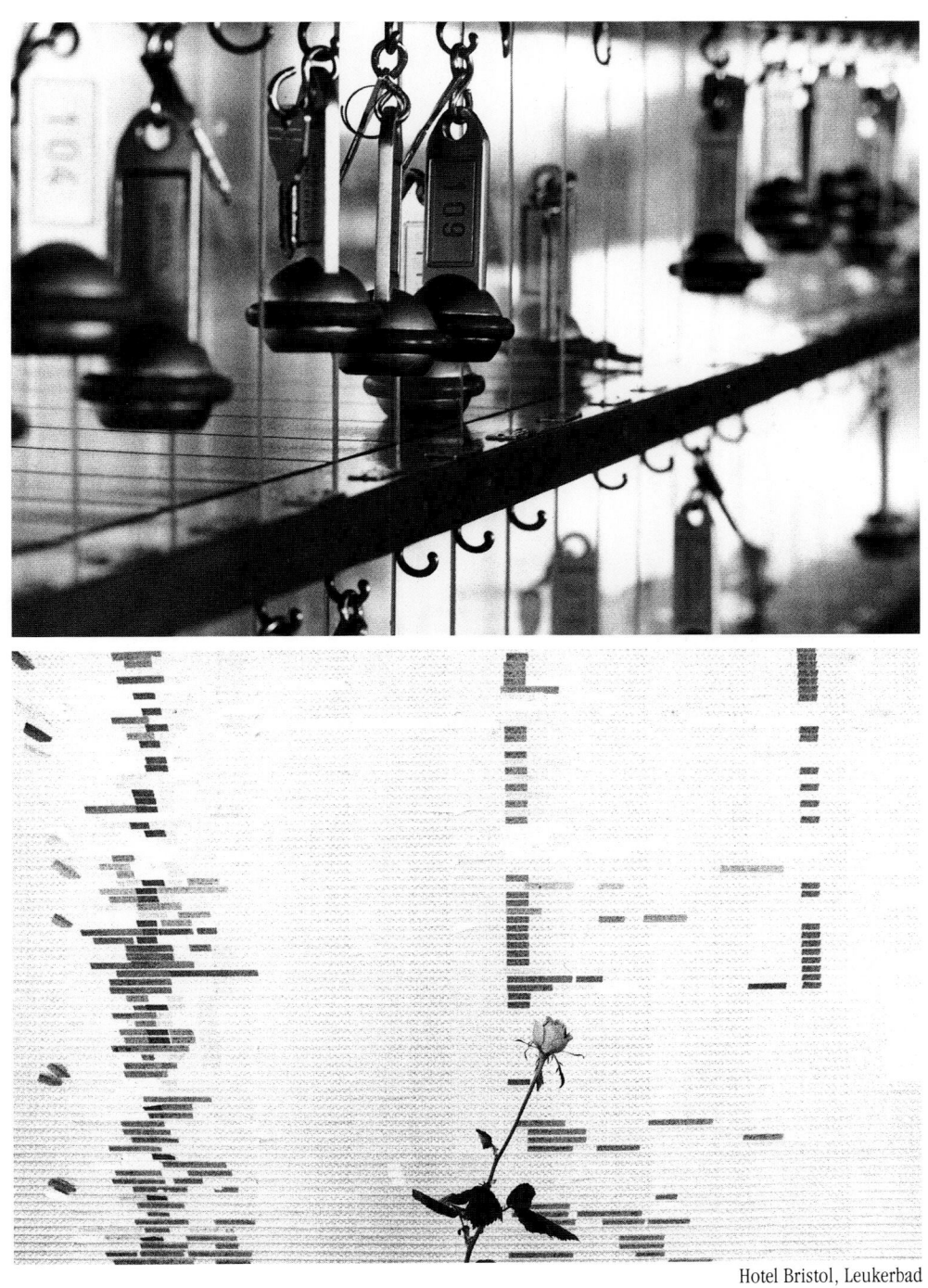

54

Hotel Principe Leopoldo, Lugano

Hotel Haus Paradies, I

Relais Châteaux Hôtel Giardino, Ascona

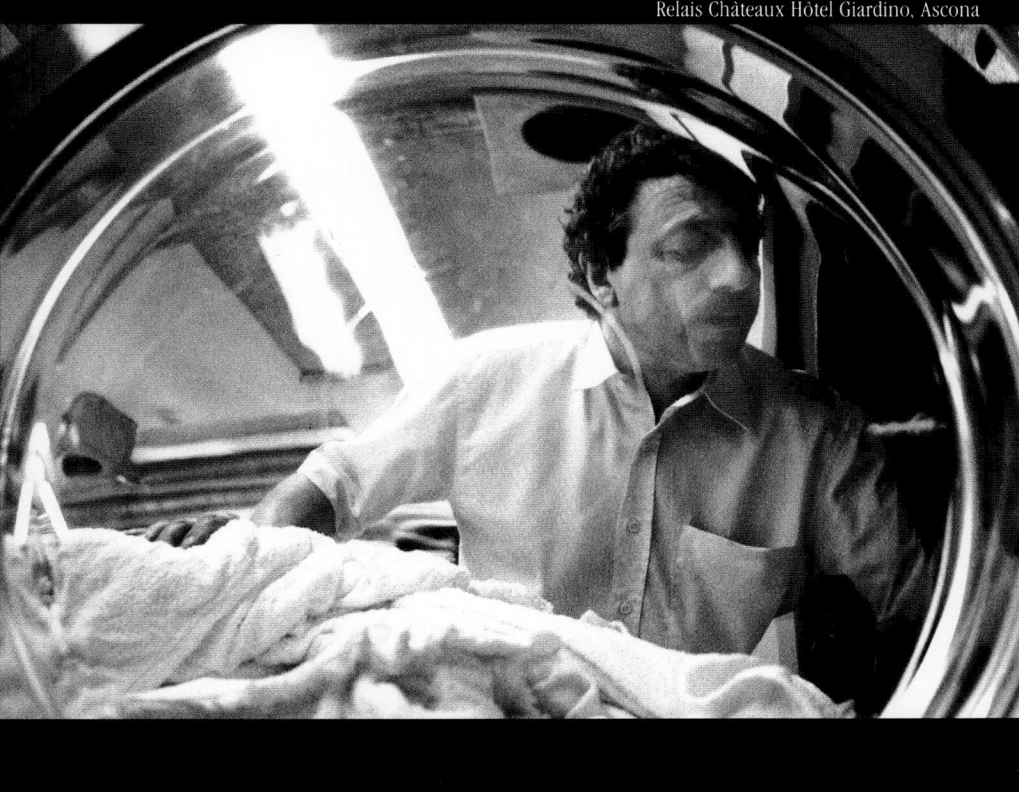

Doris Gisler Truog. Geboren 1928 in Zürich mit dem Vorsatz, Journalistin zu werden. Nach der kaufmännischen Ausbildung startete Doris Gisler als Redaktionssekretärin beim «Schweizer Heim», wo sie zwei Jahre später die Moderedaktion übernahm. Sie war als freie Journalistin tätig, bevor sie den ersten entscheidenden Auftrag der Schweiz. Käseunion erhielt, der den eigentlichen Berufswechsel zur Public-Relations-Beraterin einleitete und zu einer über dreissigjährigen Zusammenarbeit führte. Mit ihrem Mann Kaspar Gisler führte sie eine der grössten und bedeutendsten Schweizer Werbe- und PR-Agenturen. Nach dem Unfalltod von Kaspar Gisler 1971 nahm sie die Rolle als Mutter ihrer beiden Töchter Karin und Meret sowie als Geschäftsführerin der Agentur engagiert und erfolgreich wahr. Seit dem schrittweisen Verkauf der Agentur an die amerikanische Agenturkette BBDO und an führende Mitarbeiter, zog sie sich 1983 ganz von der aktiven Mitarbeit bei Gisler & Gisler zurück. Mit ihrem Ehemann Dr. med. Arnold Truog lebt Doris Gisler heute in Meilen. Neben der liebevollen Pflege des Königspudels Babar, der Katze Babuschka und den beiden Papageien, sammelt sie Hände und Händchen aller Art, farbige Gläser und zeitgenössische Kunst.

Von der Freude, Gast zu sein

Von jeher haben Hotels aller Art eine fast unwiderstehliche Anziehungskraft auf mich ausgeübt, und zu den Beglückungen meines Lebens gehört, dass ich in so vielen der schönsten von ihnen kürzere oder längere Zeit zu Gast sein durfte. Schon die Ankunft in der Halle, das Zeremoniell an der Reception, die Neugier auf das Zimmer, das für mich innert kurzer Zeit zum Zuhause wurde! Auch in Häusern, wo ich Stammgast war, habe ich mich nur selten auf eine bestimmte Zimmernummer festgelegt – zu gross war das Vergnügen, sich durch eine andere Raumeinteilung, durch einen neuen Ausblick überraschen zu lassen.

Ein Gefühl der Schwerelosigkeit überkommt mich, sobald das Gepäck im Zimmer steht und ich einen ersten Augenschein genommen habe. Sich um nichts kümmern müssen – höchstens darum, wie die diversen Knöpfe oder das Telefon funktionieren! Und – da wir in der Schweiz sind – wissen, dass sie es tun: dass die dienstbaren Geister, die sie symbolisieren, wirklich da sind und wirklich zur Verfügung stehen, und zwar innert nützlicher Frist! Höre ich da Unkenrufe? Meine Erinnerungen gehörten ins Gebiet des «Es war einmal»? Und die Schweizer Hotels seien auch nicht mehr, was sie waren? Stimmt und stimmt nicht. Nicht alle konnten sich den veränderten Ansprüchen der Gäste, um nicht zu sagen, den veränderten Gästen anpassen. Und nicht alle Probleme, die mit der Personalknappheit und den auch hier veränderten Randbedingungen fast unlösbar scheinen. Andere aber wussten, die neuen Aufgaben zu bewältigen.

Noch gibt es jene Traditionshäuser, die nicht wanken und nicht weichen und einen Standard aufrecht erhalten – man weiss nicht, wie sie es schaffen –, der bewundernswert ist und Touristen aus der ganzen Welt anziehen. Mit viel Aufwand, Liebe und Sachverstand wurden viele von ihnen in den letzten Jahren restauriert und den neuen Ansprüchen angepasst. Aber was wären die schönen Räume, die bevorzugten Aussichtslagen, wenn sie nicht durch die Schweizer Hoteliers und ihre Mitarbeiter mit Leben erfüllt, mit Sachkenntnis und Liebe zum Gast geführt würden!

Neben den traditionellen Häusern sind gerade in den letzten Jahren neue Hotels entstanden, welche sich durch ein besonders gastfreundliches Konzept rasch ihren Platz sichern konnten und ihre Anhänger fanden. Von grossen Fünfstern-Hotels mit internationaler Reputation bis zum gepflegten Landgasthof, der als Geheimtip gehandelt wird, sind viele der schönen in diesem Buch vereinigt – eine Hommage an die alte und neue Gastlichkeit in der Schweiz.

Wie jede Auswahl kann auch diese nicht frei sein von Zufälligkeit. So würde es mich bei jeder Vielfalt der Schweizer Hotellerie gar nicht wundern, wenn so manche Leserin, so mancher Leser noch ein Hotel oder einen Gasthof kennen würde, die sich hier würdig einzureihen wüssten. Der geneigte Leser hat die Wahl: den Geheimtip weiter still für sich zu geniessen – oder ihn an den Verleger dieses Buches weiterzugeben für eine allfällige weitere Ausgabe. Ich auf jeden Fall freue mich, dass das schweizerische Gastgewerbe immer wieder zu neuen Höhenflügen fähig ist und lasse mich von einer gelegentlichen schlechten Erfahrung nicht zu einem pessimistischen Gesamturteil verleiten. Der weit gereiste Gast wird immer wieder beeindruckt sein von den vielen liebevollen Details, mit denen sein Aufenthalt in einem der herausragenden Schweizer Gasthöfe verschönt wird. Viel zu wenig denken wir daran, dass wir auch als Ortsansässige in den vielen attraktiven Hotel-Restaurants willkommen sind – sei es im pompösen Saal eines Palace oder in der gemütlichen Gastwirtschaft eines Landgasthofes. Jedesmal nehmen wir dabei auch ein wenig Ferienstimmung mit – und vielleicht den Wunsch, wieder einmal für ein paar Tage da Gast zu sein, wo sich noch immer die verwöhntesten Feriengäste aus aller Welt wohl fühlen – in einem Schweizer Hotel.

Doris Gisler Truog

Doris Gisler Truog. Born in Zurich in 1928 with the aim of becoming a journalist. After a commercial training she began work as an editorial secretary for the periodical "Schweizer Heim", where she took over the post of Fashion Editor two years later. She then became a freelance journalist before receiving her first and decisive assignment from the Swiss Cheese Union, which initiated a change of profession to a public relations consultant and a period of cooperation that lasted over thirty years. With her husband Kaspar Gisler she now headed one of the largest and most prestigious Swiss advertising and public relations agencies. After Kaspar Gisler had been killed in an accident in 1971, she successfully continued the two jobs of bringing up her two daughters Karin and Meret and running the agency as business manager. In 1983, when the agency had been sold step by step to the American BBDO chain and to leading staff members, she withdrew completely from active participation in Gisler & Gisler. She now lives in Meilen with her physician husband, Dr Arnold Truog. She looks after her standard poodle Babar, her cat Babuschka and her two parrots, and collects hands of all kinds, objects in coloured glass and modern art.

The Joy of Being a Guest

Hotels of all kinds have always had an almost irresistible attraction for me, and it is one of the gratifications of my life that I have had the opportunity to spend longer or shorter periods as a guest in so many of the finest of them. The experience begins with my arrival in the lounge, the ceremony at the reception desk and my curiosity about my room, which will very quickly become my home from home. Even in hotels in which I have been a regular guest I have rarely asked for a particular room: the pleasure of being surprised by a different room layout and a different view has always been too great.

I get a feeling of weightlessness when my luggage is in the room and I have had a first look round. What a joy not to have bother about anything, or at most about how the various push-buttons and the telephone work. Since we are in Switzerland, we know that they will work, that the ministering spirits that they symbolize really are there, and available without delay. Do I hear protests? Voices saying that my memories belong to a once-upon-a-time world? And that even Swiss hotels are no longer what they used to be? That's both right and wrong. Not all hotels have managed to adapt to the changed requirements of their guests, or we might perhaps even say to the changed guests. Or to solve all the problems that shortage of staff and the altered attendant circumstances sometimes make appear almost unsolvable. Others, however, have succeeded in facing the new challenges.

There are still those traditional establishments that never waver and never give up, and that maintain a standard—one hardly knows how—that is simply admirable and attracts tourists from all over the world. Many of them have been renovated with a good deal of love, effort and insight in recent years and thus adapted to modern requirements. But what use would handsome rooms and fine views be if they were not filled with life by Swiss hoteliers and their staff, and run with expertise and a caring attitude to the guests? Alongside these traditional houses recent years have seen the rise of new hotels that have won devotees and established their claims by a special brand of hospitality. Many of the best of them are represented in this book, from big five-star hotels with an international reputation to the well-run country inn with a good name among connoisseurs; homage is thus paid to the new as well the old hospitality in Switzerland.

Like any other choice, the selection of hotels for inclusion in this book has not been entirely free from fortuitousness. Seeing how varied Swiss hotels are, it would not surprise me if many readers knew of other houses that would have deserved inclusion. Such readers now have their own choice: either to keep the name of the hotel jealously to themselves or to pass it on to the publishers of this book, so that it may be considered for a later edition. Personally I am happy to know that the Swiss hotel trade is always capable of new top-line achievements, and I do not let the occasional disappointment lead to general pessimism. The travelled guest will always be impressed by the many thoughtful details calculated to enhance his or her stay in one of the first-rank Swiss hotels. We often tend to overlook the fact that even as non-guests we are most welcome in the many attractive hotel restaurants, whether in the opulent hall of a palace hotel or in the cosy restaurant of a country inn. A visit will always inject a little of the holiday spirit, and perhaps a wish to be a guest again for a few days in a place where even pampered globe-trotters feel so well looked after—in a Swiss hotel.

Hotel Chasa Capòl, Santa Maria

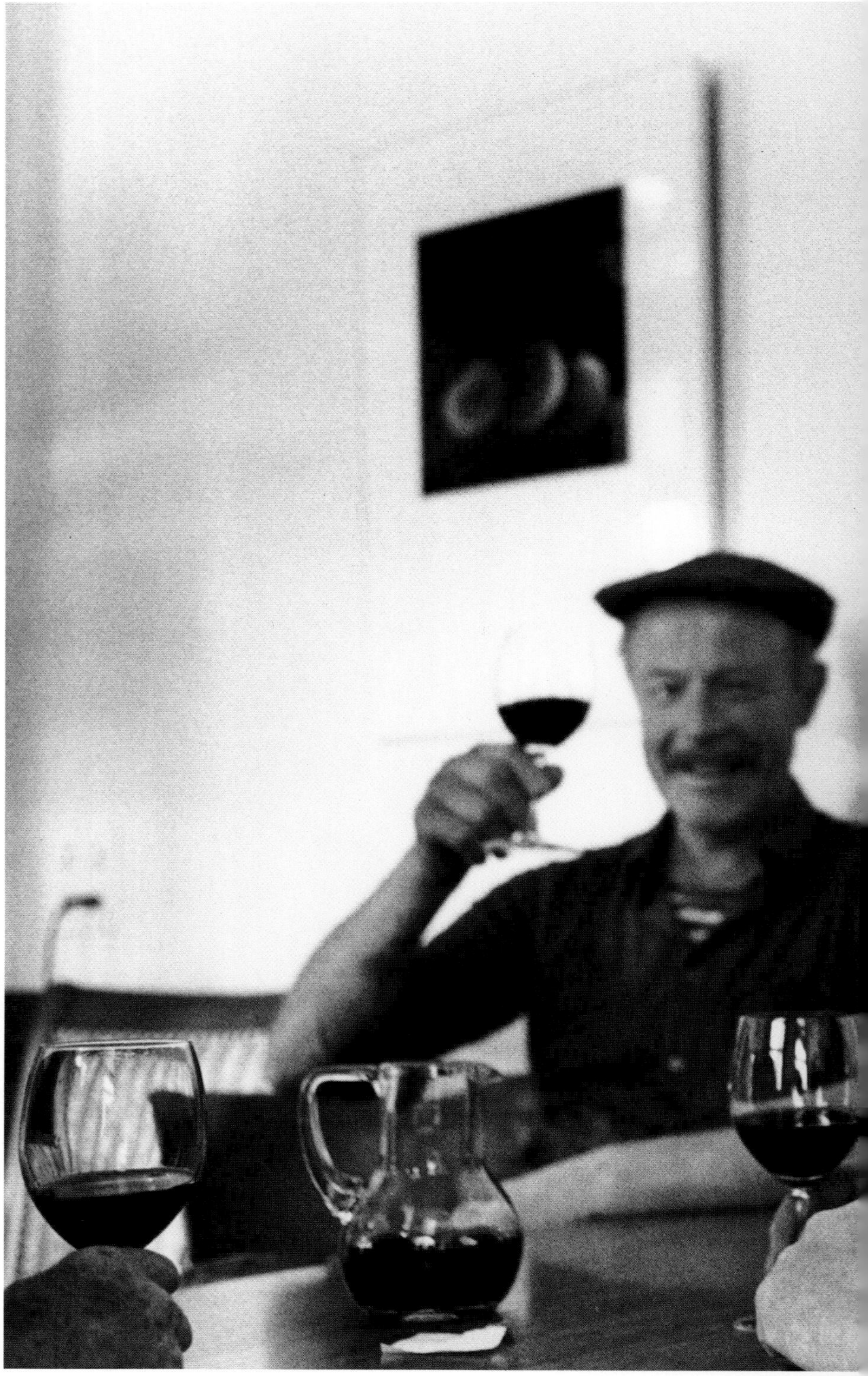

Hôtel de la Gare, Le Noirmont

Hotel Europe, Davos

Hotel Europe, Davos

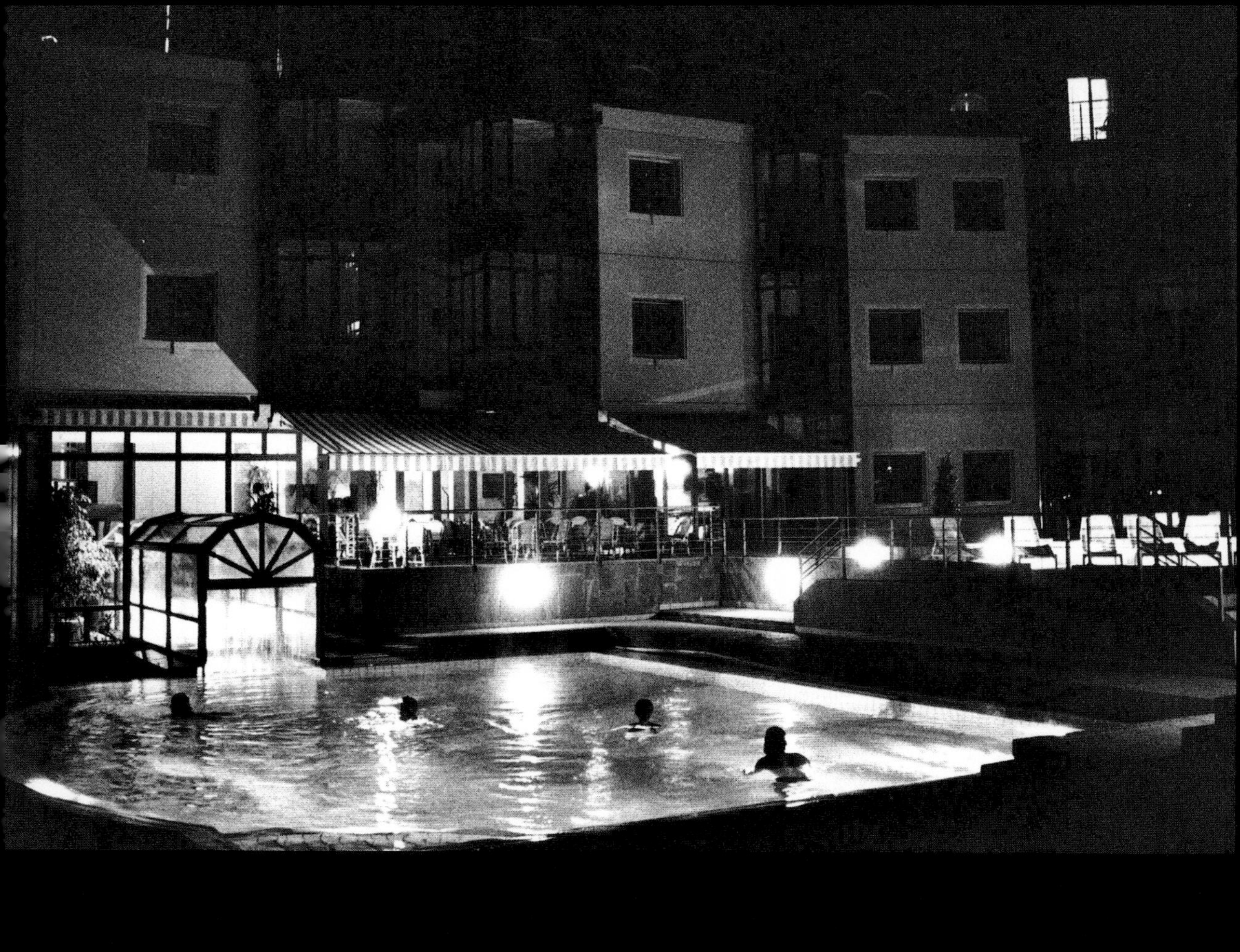

Grand Hôtel des Bains, Yverdon-les-Bains

67

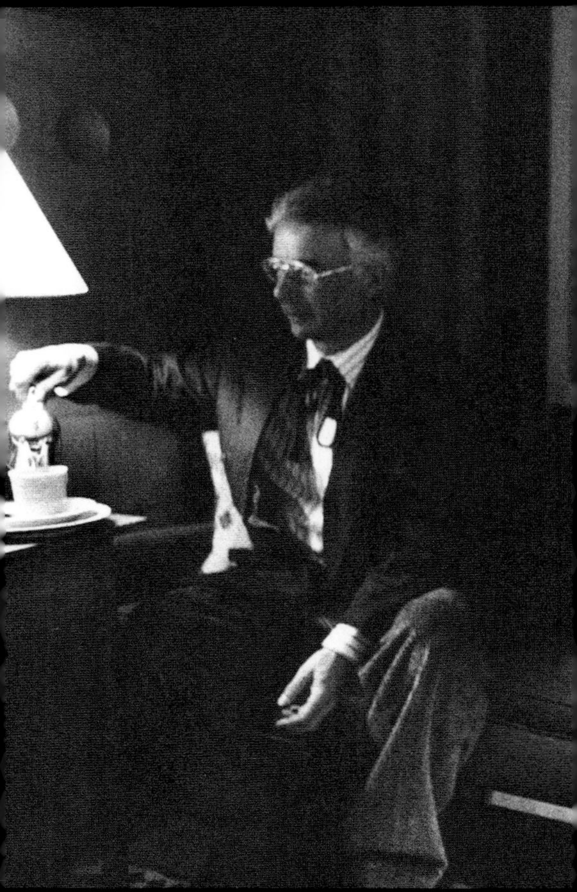

Hotel Haus Paradies, Ftan

Hôtel de la Gare, Le Noirmont

Hotel Europe, Davos

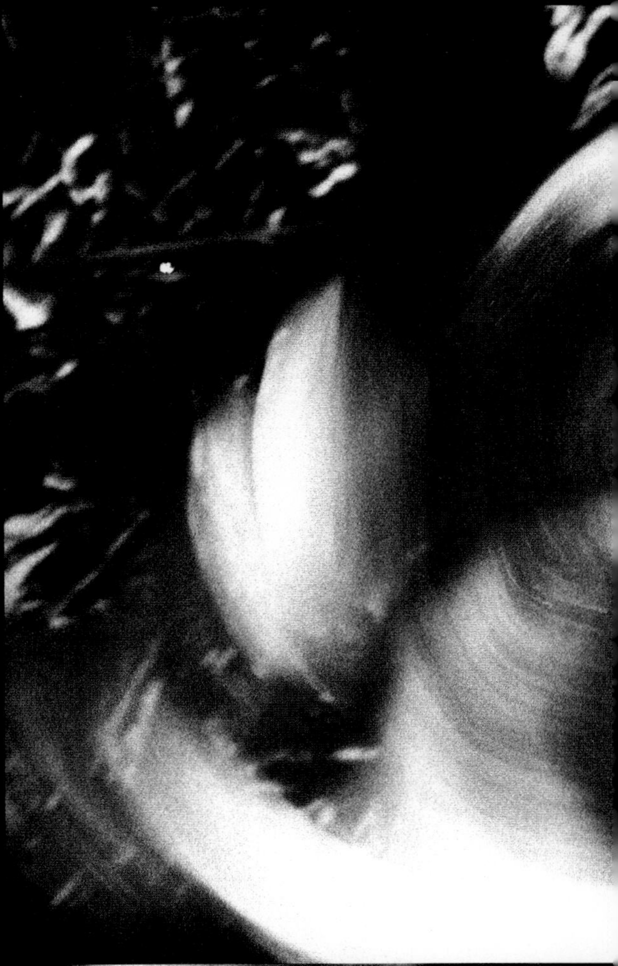

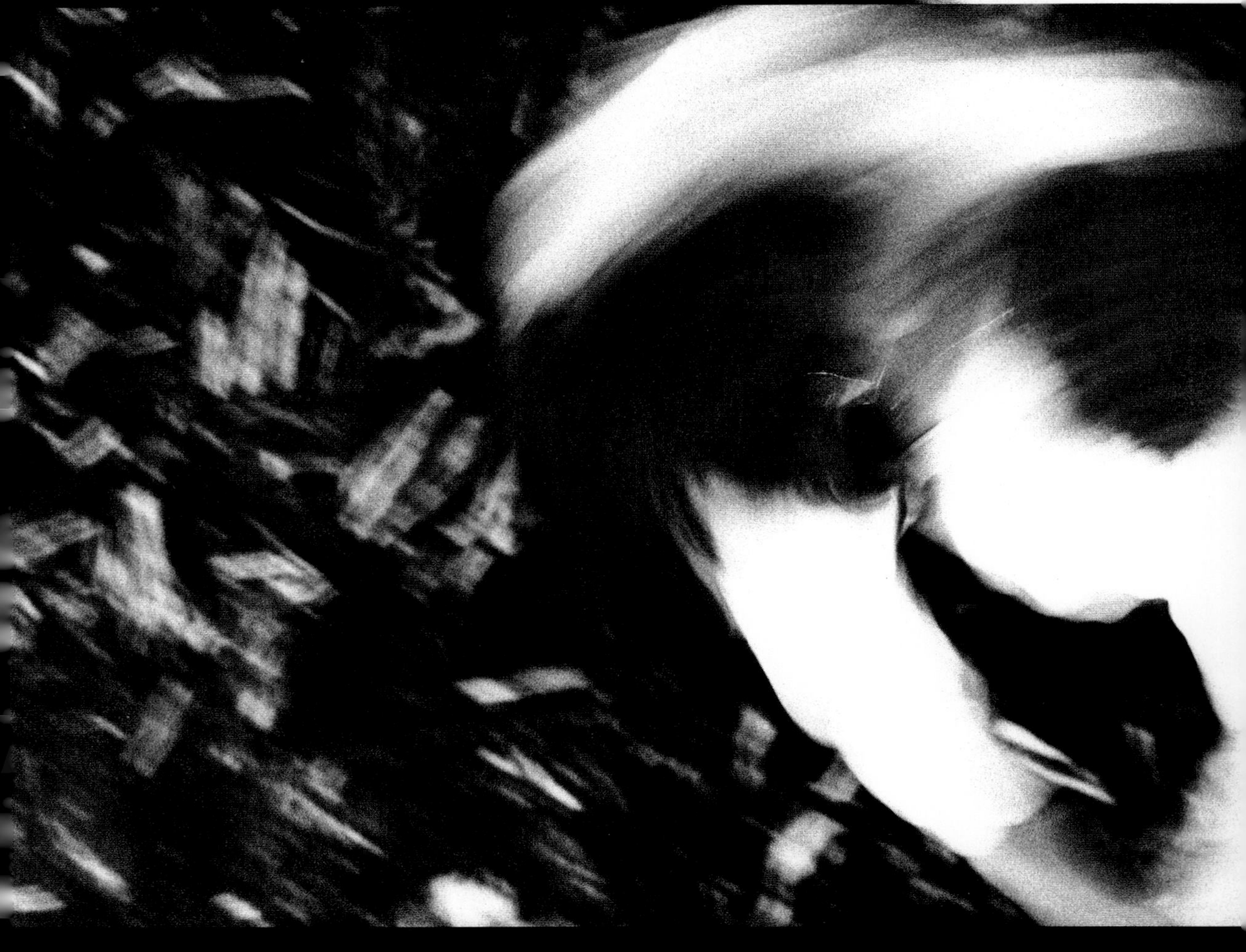

Hotel Chasa Capòl, Santa Maria

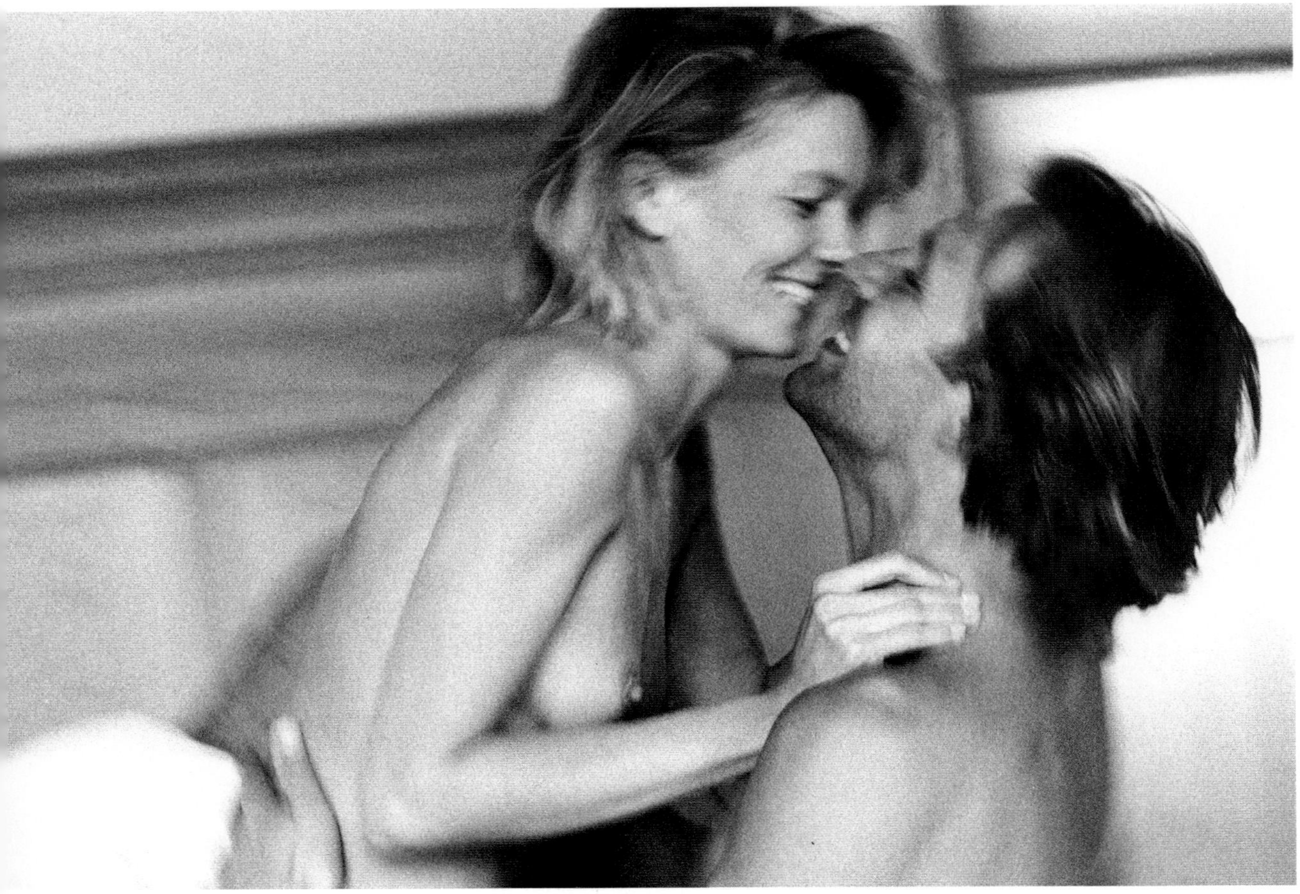

Hôtel Le Vieux Manoir au Lac, Murten

Christoph Borer. Geboren 1965 in Biel. Mogelte oder besser zauberte sich durch die Schulen bis an die Universität Bern. Da brach er nach kurzer Zeit das Studium der holden Mathematik ab, um sich für alle Zeit der schon als Sechsjähriger entdeckten Leidenschaft Zauberei zu widmen. Heute ist er als Zauberer, Träumer und Lebenskünstler auf der ganzen Welt – Hamburg, Rom, Paris, London, New York, Moskau – unterwegs. Bei sechs Zauberwettbewerben gewann er jedes Mal den ersten Preis. Während den letzten zwei Jahren wirkte er an über zwanzig Fernsehauftritten in sechs Ländern mit.
«Ich liebe es, Menschen zu verzaubern. Die Zauberkunst ermöglicht ein intensives Erleben von tiefen Gefühlen: Freude, Staunen, Lachen, Liebe. In *dieser Welt* ist das Unmögliche möglich, das Paradoxe normal und jeder Traum Realität. Viva la Magia!»

Zwischen beiden Welten

«Darf ich Ihren Ausweis sehen?» meint misstrauisch die Empfangsdame, als sie bei meiner Ankunft den Beruf «Zauberer» liest. Sie mustert gründlich meinen Pass, findet aber nichts Verdächtiges. Und da er gültig und echt schweizerisch ist, findet sich schliesslich ein Zimmer für mich. Den Pass behält sie zur Sicherheit. «Sie bekommen ihn morgen nach dem Bezahlen zurück.» Eine kleine Episode, derer ich mich immer wieder gerne erinnere. Ich will mich damit nicht beklagen. Erstens geniesst die Empfangsdame mein volles Verständnis, zweitens sind solche Begebenheiten selten.

Meine Beziehung zum Hotel ist vielfältig. Manchmal dient es mir als reine Schlafstätte – ich komme spät abends an und ziehe am nächsten Morgen weiter. Oft aber komme ich in viel engeren Kontakt, da ich im Haus auftrete, von Gästen oder vom Hotel aus engagiert. Dies schafft mir eine persönliche Beziehung – nicht zuletzt zu den Angestellten. Ich darf ein bisschen hinter die Kulissen gucken, ich erfahre, welcher Gast welche Marotte hat, warum der Koch kein Wort mit der Kellnerin wechselt, warum in einigen Zimmern die Gardinen nicht erneuert werden. Auch während meines Auftrittes gewinne ich oft gleichzeitig Einblick in beide Welten, die hinter und die vor dem Vorhang. So vergesse ich nie jene Silvesternacht im Fünf-Stern-Hotel: Die Mahlzeit wurde mir in der Kantine serviert, und das Essen war alles andere als ein Genuss. Aber es wurde gescherzt, herumgealbert und völlig spontan ein kleines Fest gefeiert. Dann ging ich hinauf zu den edlen Gästen, um sie zwischen den sechs Gängen eines Erst-Klasse-Menüs mit Zauberei ein bisschen zu amüsieren. Aber trotz der delikaten Speisen, der Musik, der gebotenen Unterhaltung und der tollen Dekoration wollte keine richtig fröhliche Stimmung aufkommen; schon eher eine Art gezwungene Lustigkeit. Auftretende Künstler werden vom Hotel im allgemeinen gut behandelt, aber wenn Du nach der Vorstellung schlafen gehen willst, merkst Du, dass es auch im besten Hotel immer ein kleines, «leider gerade noch nicht renoviertes» Zimmer gibt. Na ja, auch das gehört zum Leben zwischen beiden Welten. Denke ich an Hotels, überkommt mich immer ein spezielles Gefühl, das jeder herumreisende, auftretende Künstler kennt.

Nach dem erfolgreichen Auftritt gehst Du ins Hotel zurück, erschöpft, leer, sinnend. Du sitzt im Zimmer, alleine. Du möchtest mit einem Menschen sprechen, eine Frau umarmen, mit jemandem scherzen. Aber Hotelzimmer sind Einzelzellen. Kontakte zu anderen sind nicht möglich. Vielleicht dringt kurz das helle Lachen zweier glücklicher Menschen durch die dünne Wand. Aber das stimmt Dich auch nicht fröhlicher. Du gehst hinunter, in die Hotelbar. Doch auch ein Gin Tonic kann Deine Stimmung nicht heben. Widerstrebend schleichst Du aufs Zimmer zurück. Du denkst an den heutigen Auftritt, an den Applaus, an die Menschen, die mit Dir gesprochen haben. Einer bat sogar um ein Autogramm. Eine hübsche Frau hat Dich deutlich mehr als nur freundlich angelächelt. Doch all dies lässt Dich den Gegensatz der Leere des Augenblicks nur noch deutlicher wahrnehmen. Schliesslich schläfst Du ein. Der nächste Tag kommt. Die Sonne scheint. Du gehst hinaus, Du siehst die lachenden Menschen, Du fühlst Dich blendend. Du gehst gut essen und bist glücklich. Dann reist Du weiter. Der nächste Veranstalter erwartet Dich, die nächste Show, das nächste Hotel.

Christoph Borer

Christoph Borer. Born in Bienne in 1965. Scraped or rather bluffed his way through school up to Berne University, where he soon gave up his study of mathematics to devote himself permanently to his passion for conjuring, which he had discovered at the age of six. Today he travels all over the world—Hamburg, Paris, London, New York, Moscow—as a magician, dreamer and hedonist. He won first prize every time in six conjuring competitions. In the last two years he has appeared on television over twenty times in six countries. "I love putting a spell on people. Wizardry is a way to the intense experience of profound feelings: joy, astonishment, laughter, love. In *this world* the impossible becomes possible, the paradoxical is normal and every dream reality. Viva la Magia!"

Between the Two Worlds

"May I see your identity papers?" says the receptionist suspiciously on my arrival, having just read my profession: "Magician". She scrutinizes the passport, but can find nothing wrong with it. And since it is valid and genuinely Swiss, she finally finds a room for me. But she keeps the passport for safety's sake. "You'll get it back tomorrow when you pay your bill." A little episode I like to hark back to. Not that I am complaining. Firstly, I quite understand the receptionist; and secondly, such incidents are rare.

My relations with hotels are multifold. Sometimes a hotel is just a place to sleep—I arrive late at night and move on the next morning. But frequently the contact is much closer, as I do a performance in the house, having been engaged by guests or by the hotel management. This gives me a personal connection, in particular with the staff. I am allowed to peep behind the scenes, I find out the idiosyncrasies of the guests, why the cook isn't speaking to the waitress, or why the curtains are not being changed in some rooms. During my show I often get a view of both worlds, that behind and that in front of the curtain. I will never forget a New Year's night in a certain five-star hotel. I was served a meal in the canteen, and there was nothing Lucullan about it. But there was a lot of joking and fooling around, and a small party was spontaneously celebrated. Then I went up to the honoured guests to entertain them a little with my wizardry between the six courses of a first-class menu. But in spite of the delicious food, the music, the wonderful decorations and my attempts at diversion, there was not much gaiety in the air; at most a kind of forced amusement. Entertainers are usually well treated by hotels, but when you retire after the performance, you find that even in the best hotel you have been given a small and unattractive room, one that is often "just about to be renovated". Oh well, that is no doubt part of the life between the two worlds. When I think of hotels, I always get a special feeling that must be familiar to every artiste who tours around with his act.

After your performance you go to your room, exhausted, empty, meditative. There you sit alone. You would perhaps like to talk to somebody, to put your arm around a lady friend, to share a joke. But hotel rooms are a form of solitary confinement, contacts with other human beings are not on the agenda. Sometimes the laughter of two happier guests may be heard through the thin walls. But that doesn't cheer you up either. You can go down to the hotel bar, but a gin tonic doesn't usually do much for your spirits. So you reluctantly return to your room. You think of your performance, of the applause, of the people you spoke to. One of them even wanted an autograph. There was an attractive woman who smiled at you with demonstrative warmth. All only underlines the emptiness that now surrounds you. You finally get to sleep. On the following day the sun is shining. You go out, you see people laughing, you feel fine. You go and have a good meal and are happy. Then you go on your way. The next organizer is waiting for you, the next show, the next hotel.

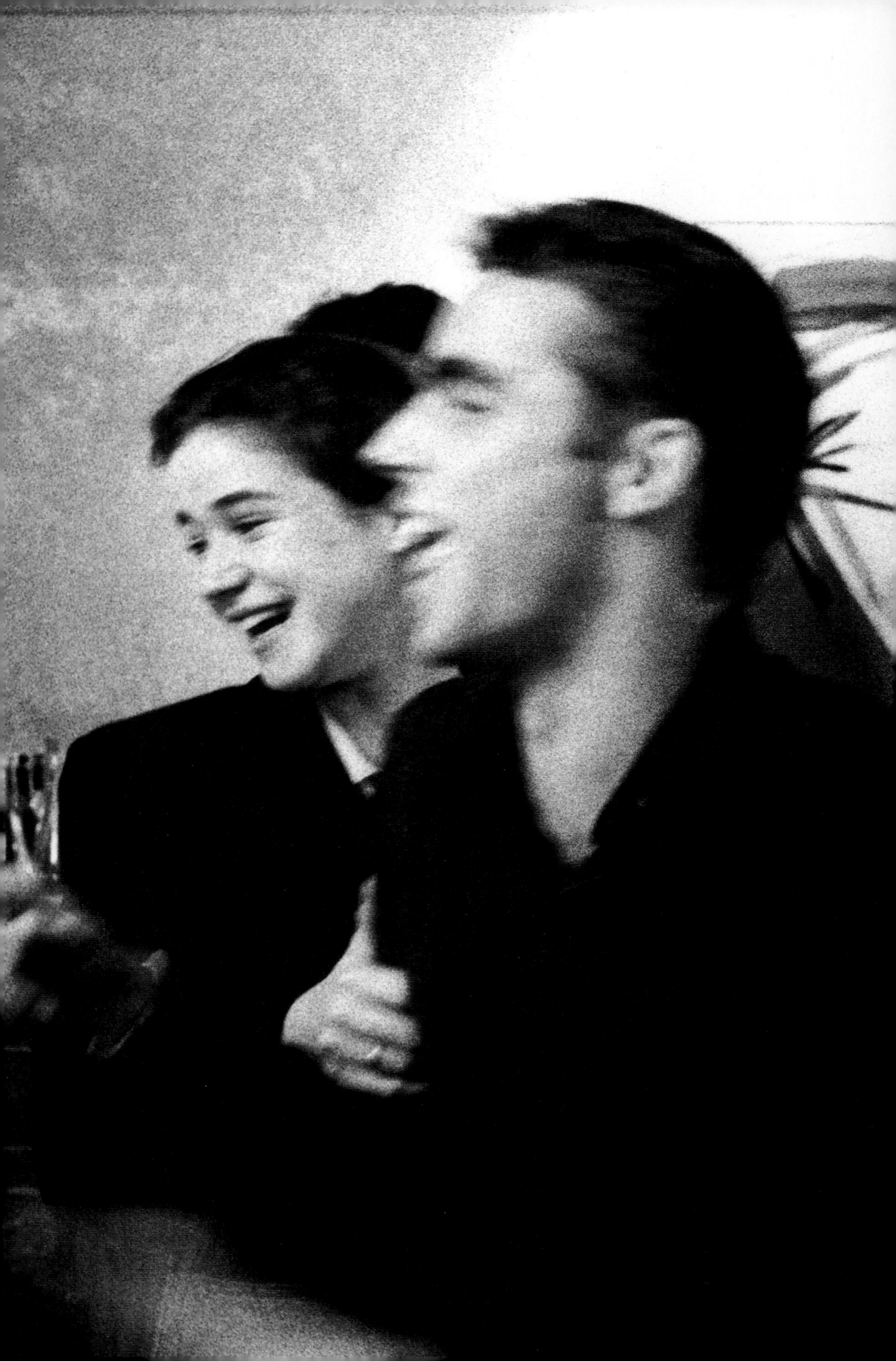

Hôtel de la Gare, Le Noirmont

80

Hotel Lago di Lugano, Bissone

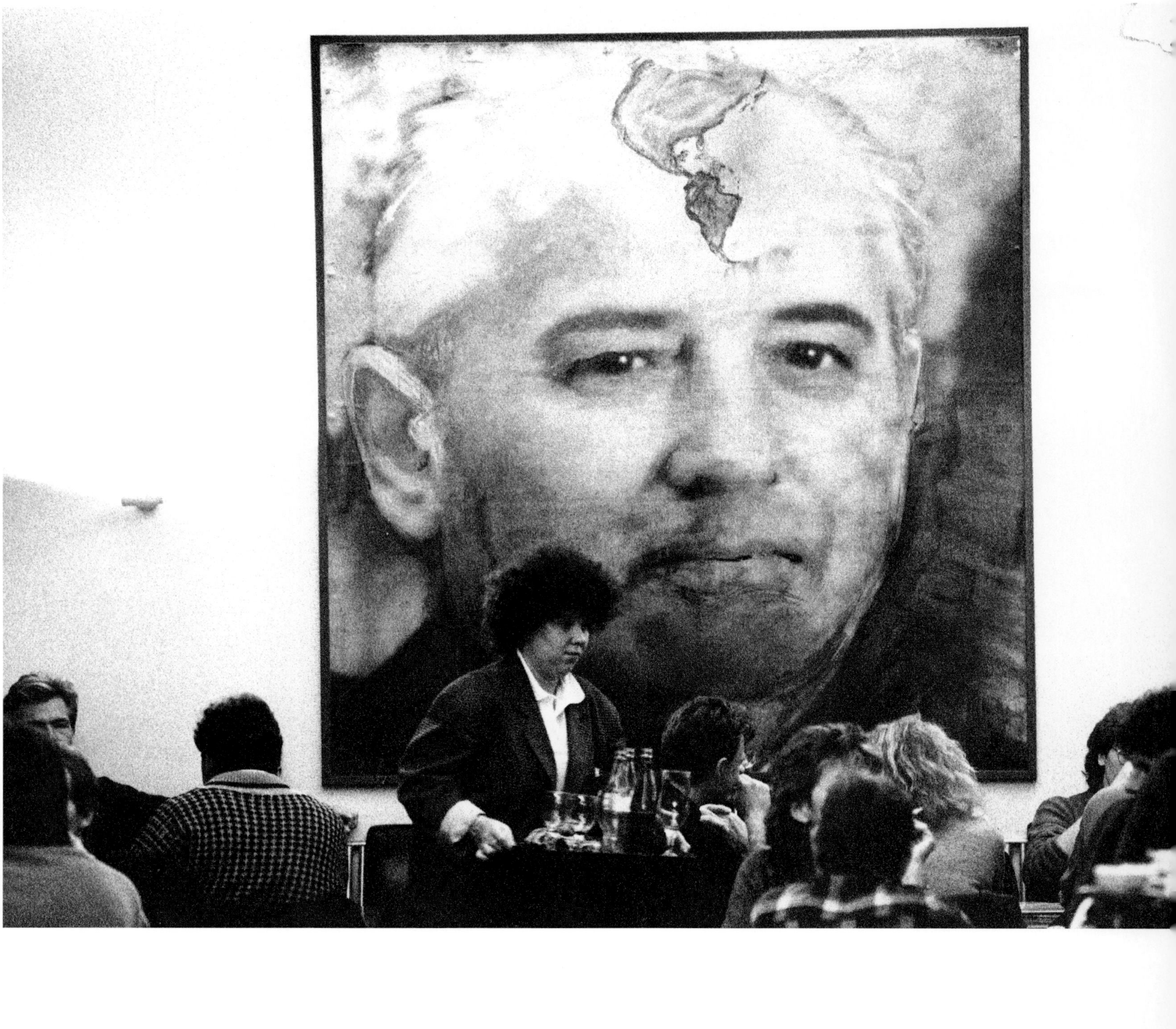

Hotel Europe, Davos

Hotel Principe Leopoldo, Lugano

83

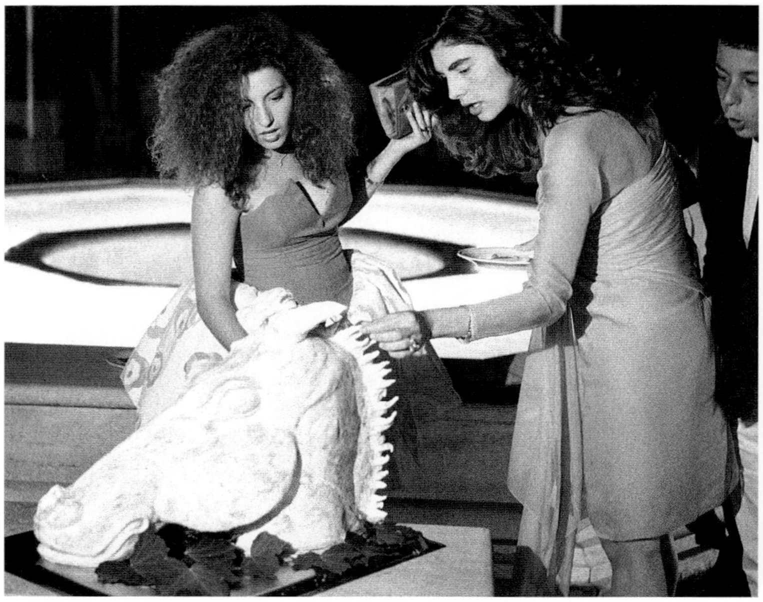

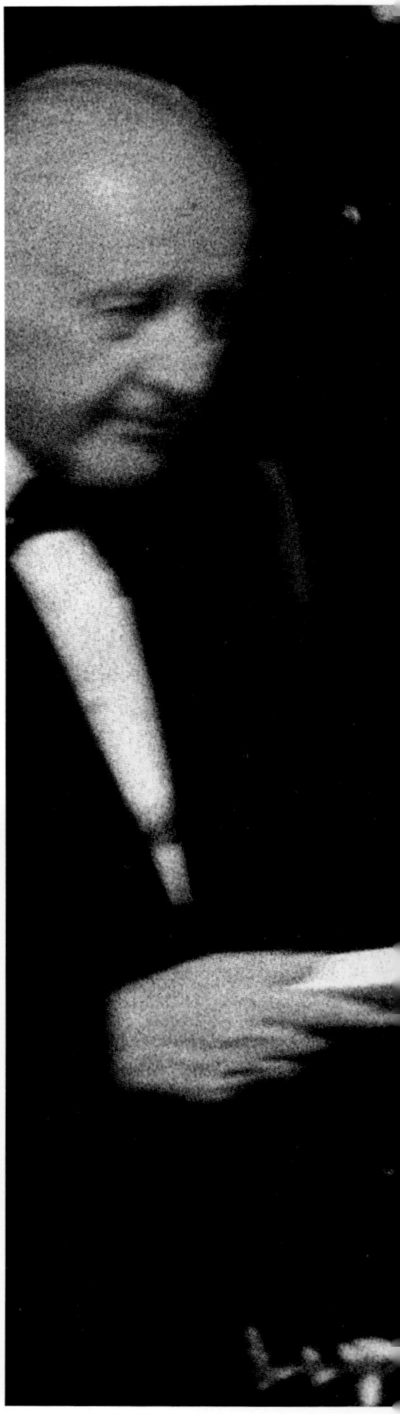

Hotel Principe Leopoldo, Lugano

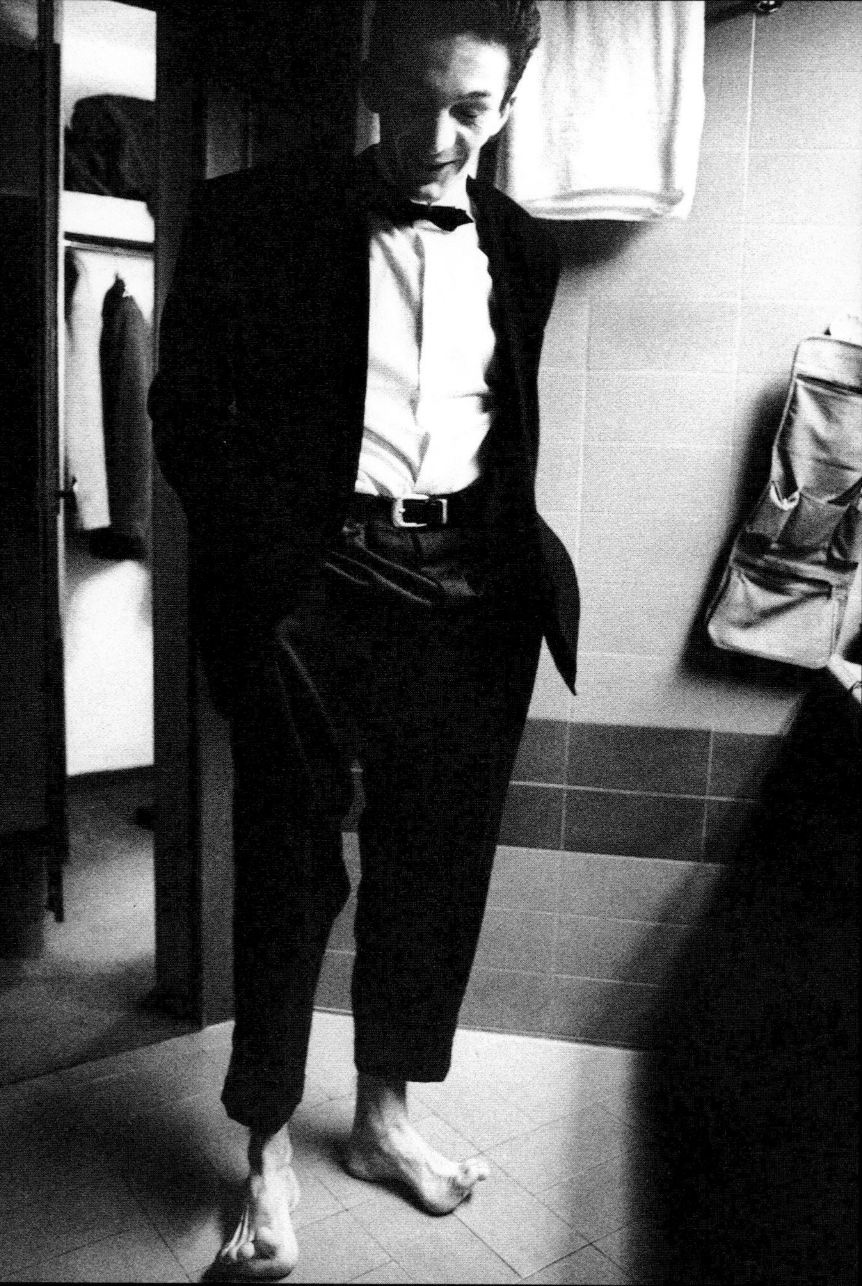

Hotel Chesa Guardalej, Champfèr

88

Hotel Eden, Arosa

Märchenhotel Bellevue, Braunwald

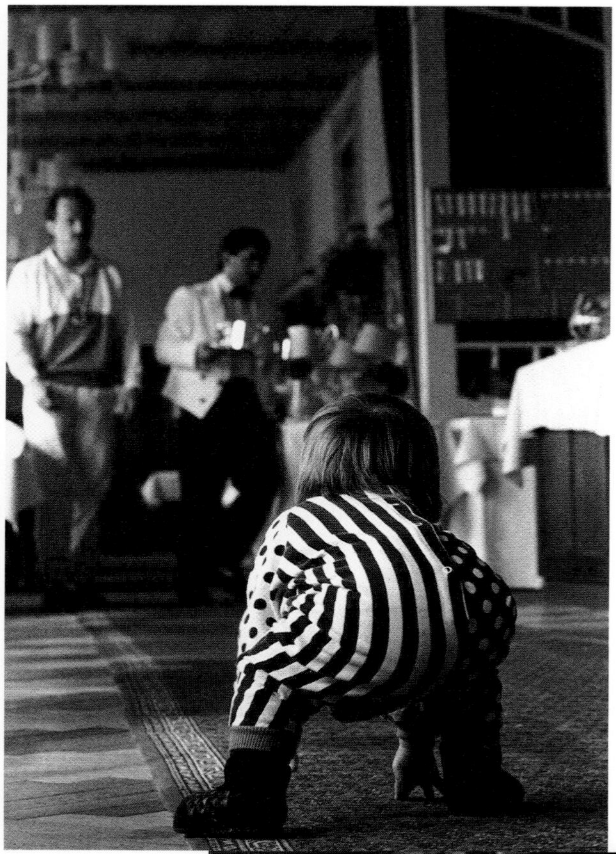

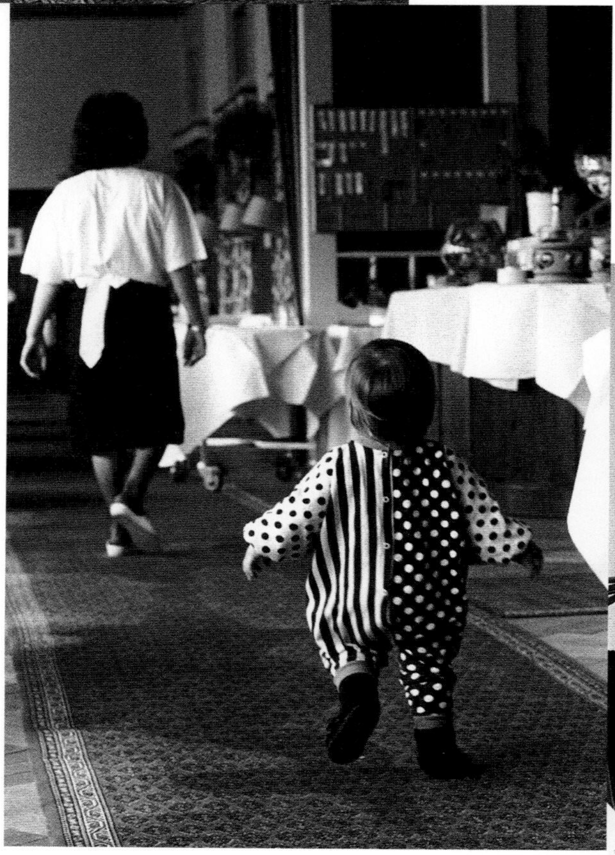

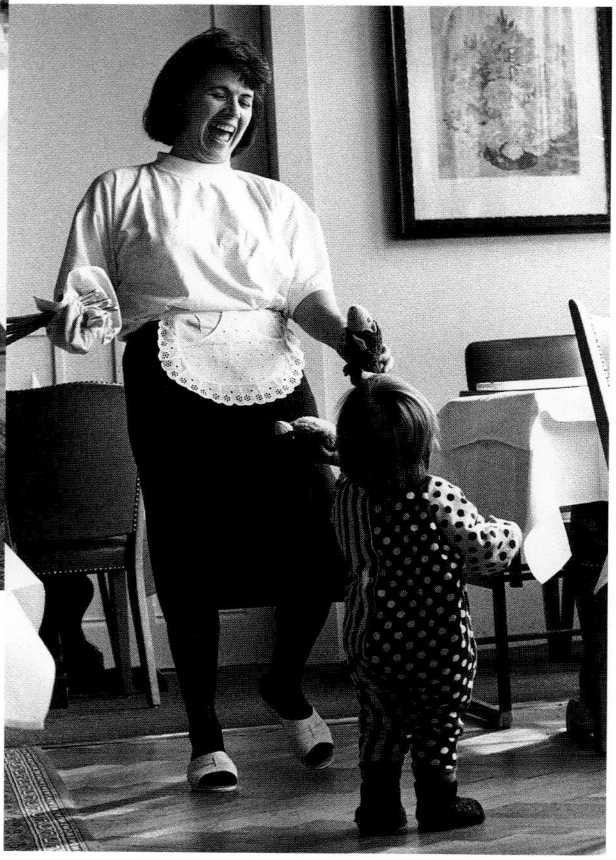

Märchenhotel Bellevue, Braunwald

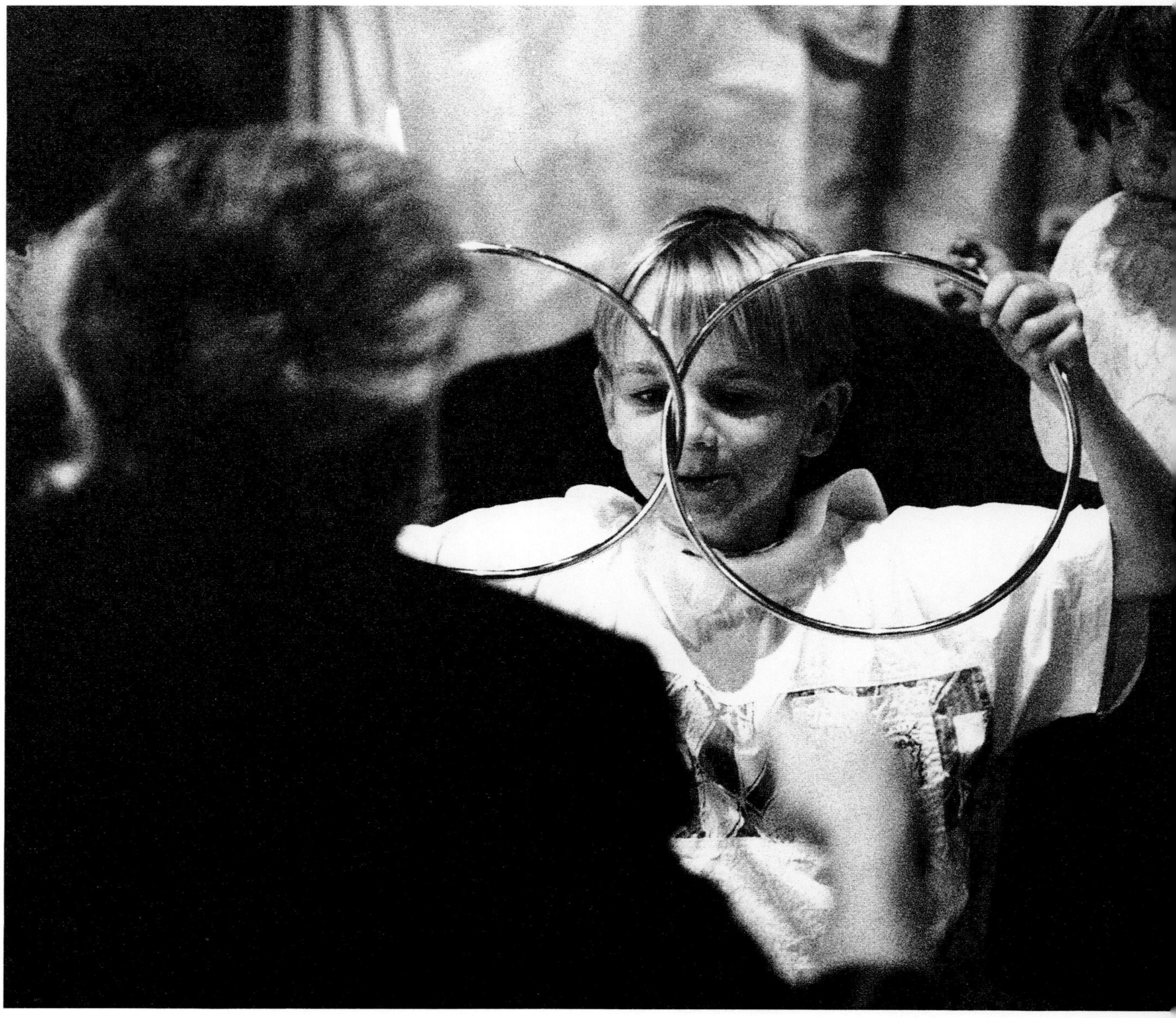

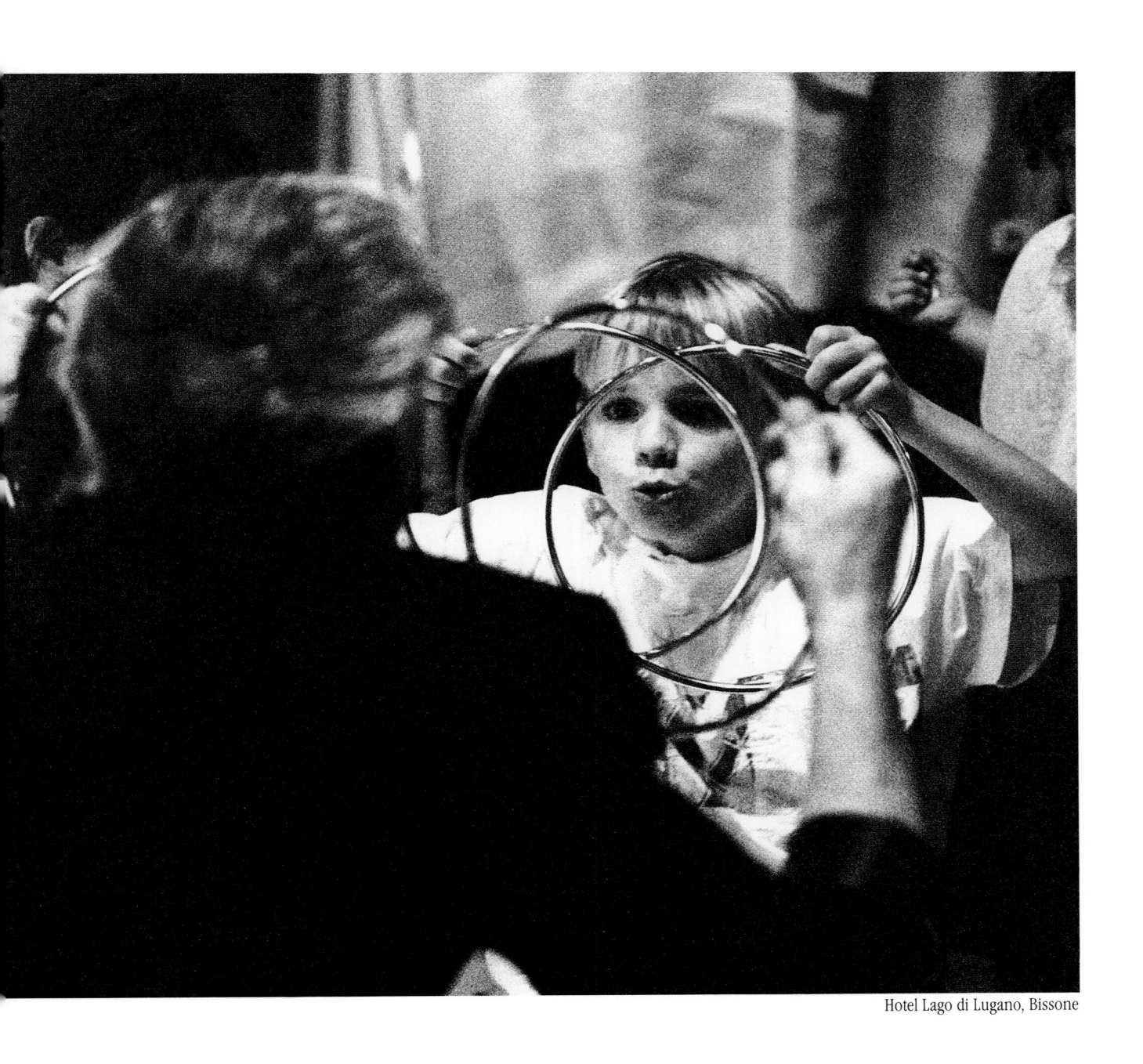

Hotel Lago di Lugano, Bissone

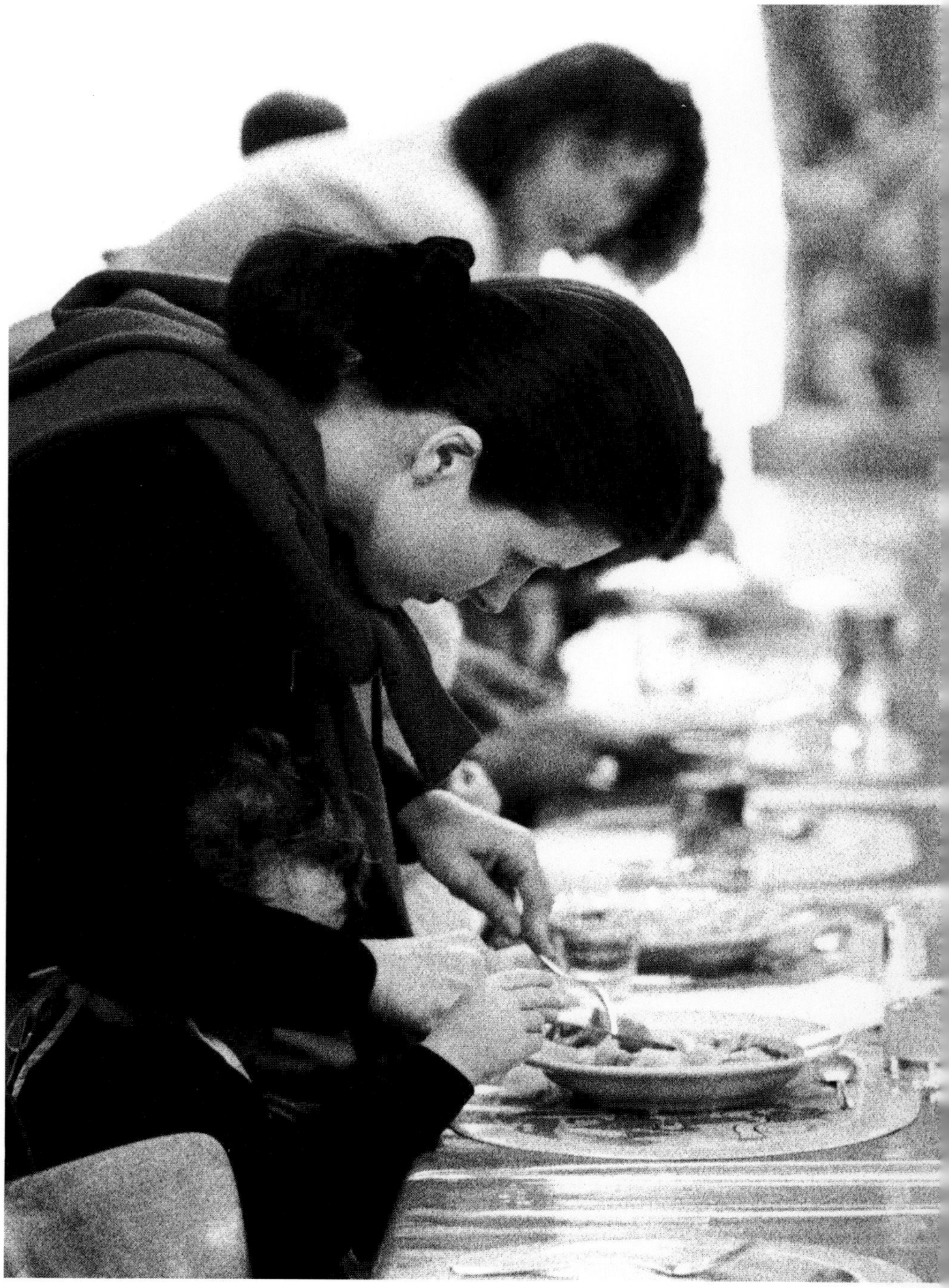

Märchenhotel Bellevue, Braunwald

Lian Maria Bauer. Geboren 1956 in München. Im Ambiente der Kunst- und Künstlerstadt schliesst sie 1981 die Deutsche Meisterschule für Mode mit Diplom ab. Als Kostümbildnerin für Filmproduktionen verwirklicht Lian Bauer erstmals ihre Imaginationen. 1982 gründet sie die Firma «Die Mappe – Werkstatt für Design». 1985 kommt ein Einrichtungsgeschäft mit eigenen Möbeln und Beratung dazu. Zwei Jahre später wird konsolidiert und es entsteht die Firma Lian Maria Bauer – Environmentdesign. Dekorationsgestaltung für Veranstaltungen und Verkaufspräsentationen, Gestaltung von Objekteinrichtungen, Set-Design für Foto und Film und die Gestaltung von Dekorationsmaterial und Dummies. Über alle Jahre hinweg gehören Hotels und Restaurants zu Lian Bauers Kunden.

Ambiente

Während Männer in der Regel allenfalls zwischen Tag- und Abendgarderobe zu unterscheiden wissen, spielen Frauen dagegen mit den Gesetzen des Kleidens und Verkleidens, des Schmückens und Ausschmückens und bewegen sich mit meist traumwandlerischer Sicherheit auf den Pfaden der Mode. Eine Frau wechselt ihr Outfit häufiger, doch niemals ohne Grund. Der geringste Anlass erscheint ihr bedeutend genug.

Im Kampf um die Gunst des Hotelgast-Kunden spielen Luxus und Komfort nur Nebenrollen. Was zählt, ist das Erlebnis Hotelaufenthalt. Er muss der Bühne «Leben» Raum geben. Doch von einer «Lebensbühne Hotel» ist weit und breit in der ach so gediegenen Hotellerie nur wenig zu sehen. Ambiente ist Luxus und dieser wird als entscheidender Produktfaktor allenfalls mit vergoldetem Chichi und Büttenrändern an den Speisekarten verwechselt. Ein wenig Tüll kaschiert die Einfallslosigkeit, die das Management samt Personal und Gästen saisonweise durchs Jahr treibt. Dekorationen erdreisten sich, Stimmungen hervorprovozieren zu wollen, die von nichts und niemand der Anwesenden dann wirklich getragen werden. Die falsch verstandene Verkleidung schafft weder das aufwertende Ambiente, noch ist sie in der Lage, auch nur ansatzweise die Kunst des weiblichen Sich-Schmückens zu imitieren.

Als Gestalterin ist es eine meiner mit Leidenschaft und Engagement realisierten Aufgaben, für Hotels zu verschiedensten Anlässen Ambiente zu schaffen. Ambiente fängt mit der Konzeption an. Es schlägt sich im Farbklima nieder, spiegelt sich in Formen, Material und Licht und Ambiente hört mit der Gestaltung von Festen noch lange nicht auf. Der Logenplatz in der Gunst des Gastes wird heute nicht mehr auf den Schlachtplätzen der Cuisine oder im Wartesaal der Designer-Eitelkeiten geführt. Gunst ist etwas so Immaterielles, wie Ambiente – und doch spiegelt sich beides im Materiellen wieder.

Umwelt beginnt nicht erst draussen vor der Tür. Innen machen Farbkomposition und Formengestaltung einen Raum ständig präsent. Umwelt als Ambiente kann aktivieren oder durch Langeweile blockieren. Unser Unterbewusstsein nimmt davon viel mehr auf und beeinflusst unsere Stimmung viel mehr, als wir tatsächlich davon bemerken wollen.

Durch abwechslungsreiche, optische Veränderungen wird, wie in der Natur durch die Jahreszeiten, Bewegung geschaffen. Die Mimikry von Fauna und Flora dient dem Schutz und Reiz zu gleichen Teilen und ihr Wechsel schafft Raum fürs Neue. Die Kreativität des Gastes anzuregen, mit Illusionen der Erlebniswelt den Horizont zu sprengen oder die Phantasie hilfreich mit dem Erzählen «Optischer Geschichten» zu stimulieren, ist die Aufgabe, die ereignis-bezogene Dekorationen zu übernehmen haben. Der Anlässe sind genug und nicht immer muss es nur das saisonale «Frühlingszwiebelfest», «Silvesterkarpfenmenü» oder «Herbstzeitlosendinner» sein. Die Dekoration vorhandener Räumlichkeiten für Erlebnis-Abende geben dem Gast, neben einem nicht zu vergessenden Ereignis und der guten Erinnerung ans gastgebende Hotel, ein ungezwungenes Verhalten, und freie Kontakte zu anderen Gästen.

Wie eine Filmkulisse, in die sich das Hotel mit seinem Service integriert, gibt die Dekoration dem Gast das Gefühl, sich in einer vollkommen anderen Welt zu befinden. Die mittlerweile «berühmten» Feste «Das Geheimnis der Titanic», «New York 1997» oder auch «1001 Nacht» des Hotels Eden in Arosa, sind gute Beispiele dafür, wie Gäste stimuliert, verführt und zur besten Laune animiert werden können und warum sich solcherlei Ideen ausserhalb der Normalität auch lange später noch mehr als bezahlt machen.

Die Gestaltung des Kitchen Clubs gibt einen anderen Einblick in meine konzeptionelle Arbeit: Nachdem die Wintermäntel im Kühlhaus abgegeben sind, vergnügen sich die Gäste in der (nunmehr zur Diskothek umgebauten) Hotelküche. Zwischen Kartoffelschälmaschine und Salatschleuder werden die Gäste von der heissen Musik des Diskjockeys mitgerissen, dessen Thron der Nacht ein ehemaliger Grossküchenherd ist. Zu später Stunde lädt ein Riesentopf zum Spaghettikochen ein. Töpfe, Kannen und Siebe schmücken nicht nur die rohverlegten Rohre, sie sind fester Bestandteil eines gewollten Ambientes im Gesamtkonzept einer aussergewöhnlichen Discothek.

Ambiente zu schaffen ist mein Beruf. Nicht nur, weil ich es liebe, mit Farben und Formen, mit Details und ausgewählten Requisiten, Raumbilder zu schaffen, sondern auch, weil ich letztendlich selbst oft genug Gast bin und mich in einer erlebnisreichen Umwelt – dem «anspruchs-erfüllenden» Hotel – wohl fühlen möchte.

Lian Maria Bauer

Lian Maria Bauer. Born in Munich in 1956. In the environment of this city of art and artists she won a diploma in 1981 at the German fashion school. She first realized her visions as a costume designer for film productions. In 1982 she founded a company under the style of "The Portfolio—Workshop for Design". In 1985 she opened a furnishing store with her own furniture and a consulting service. Two years later a consolidation phase produced the company Lian Maria Bauer—Environment Design: design of decorations for festive occasions and sales presentations, object installations, set designs for photography and films and the design of decorative materials and dummies. Hotels and restaurant have figured prominently among her clients over the years.

Ambiente

While men can usually distinguish at best only between morning and evening wear, women like to play with the laws of dressing and changing, of make-up and accessoires, and are usually very much at home in the mazes of fashion. Women change their outfits more frequently, though never without reason. The slightest occasion will justify a change.

In the competition for the favour of hotel guests luxury and comfort are only secondary considerations. The thing that counts is the experience of a stay at a hotel. This must provide a stage for living. Yet in the hotel trade, even at its most polished, there is not a great deal to be seen of this living stage. Ambiente is a luxury, and this decisive factor is mostly understood as a measure of gold plating and deckle edges on the menus. A little tulle serves to cover up the lack of ideas that drives the management with staff and guests through the seasons. Decorations are credited with creating moods that are not really felt by any of those present. Misunderstood disguises cannot produce the real virtues of the ambiente, nor can they even begin to imitate the art of feminine self-adornment.

As a designer I am given the assignment—which I carry out with passion and commitment—to create an ambiente for occasions of many kinds in hotels. An ambiente begins as a concept. It expresses itself in the colour climate, is mirrored in forms, materials and lighting, and does not come to end with the shaping of the festivities themselves. The high places in the favour of guests are no longer won on the battlefields of the kitchen or in the waiting-room of design vanities. Favour is something as abstract as ambiente, yet both are reflected in material things.

The environment does not begin outside the door. Inside, too, colour compositions and designed forms can give a room a presence of its own. In the form of an ambiente, the environment can activate observers or block them with tedium. Our subconscious absorbs much more of it and thus affects our mood much more than we usually realize.

Movement can be generated by ever-varying optical changes, such as are engendered in nature by the seasons. The mimicry of flora and fauna serves both for protection and for excitement, and its alternation opens the doors to new experiences. The purpose of event-related decorations is to stir the creativity of guests, to open up their horizons with illusions or to support and stimulate their imagination with "optical stories". There are plenty of occasions for this: it need not always be the "spring onion festival", the "New Year carp menu" or the "autumn crocus dinner". The decoration of existing rooms for festive evenings can ensure natural conviviality among guests and unstrained contacts with each other while making for an unforgettable event and leaving favourable memories of the hotel in which it took place.

Like a film setting, in which the hotel and its service are integrated, the decorations give guests the feeling of moving in a completely different world. The now famous festivities of "The Secret of the Titanic", "New York 1997" and the "Arabian Nights" of the Eden Hotel in Arosa are good examples of the way guests can be stimulated, charmed and animated, and of how such out-of-the-normal ideas can bring much later returns.

The design of the Kitchen Club gives a further impression of my conceptual work. When their winter coats have been stowed away in the cold-storage room, the guests amuse themselves in the hotel kitchen (now converted into a disco). They are carried away, between potato peeler and salad centrifuge, by the hot music of the disc jockey, whose nocturnal throne is a massive old cooking range. When the night has worn on, a huge pot invites the dancers to a spaghetti binge. Pots, cans and sieves adorn the open-laid pipes and form an essential part of a plannend ambiente conceived as an extraordinary disco.

Creating the ambiente is my profession. Not only because I love to design room effects with shapes and colours, carefully chosen props and details, but just as much because I am often a guest myself and like to enjoy myself in an exciting environment offered by a hotel that really fulfils its guests' expectations.

Hotel Furkablick, Realp

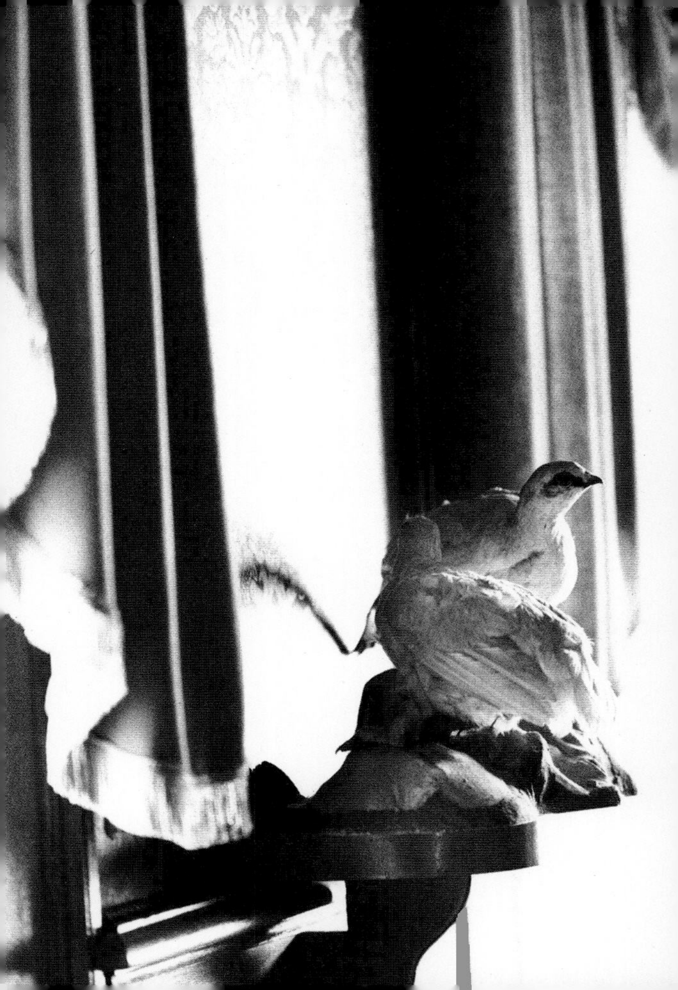

Hôtel de la Gare, Le Noirmont

Hotel Lago di Lugano, Bissone

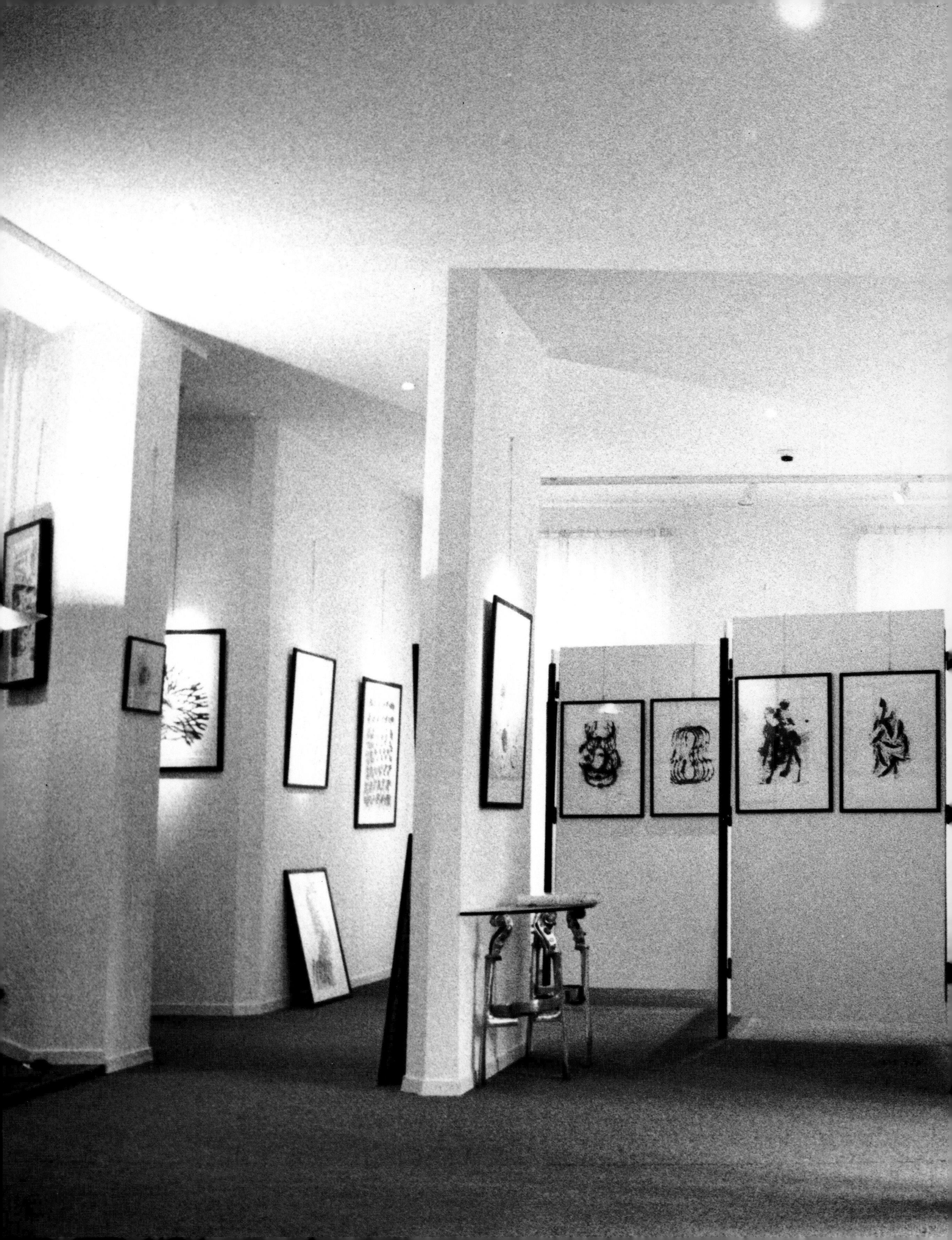

Park Hotels Waldhaus, Flims

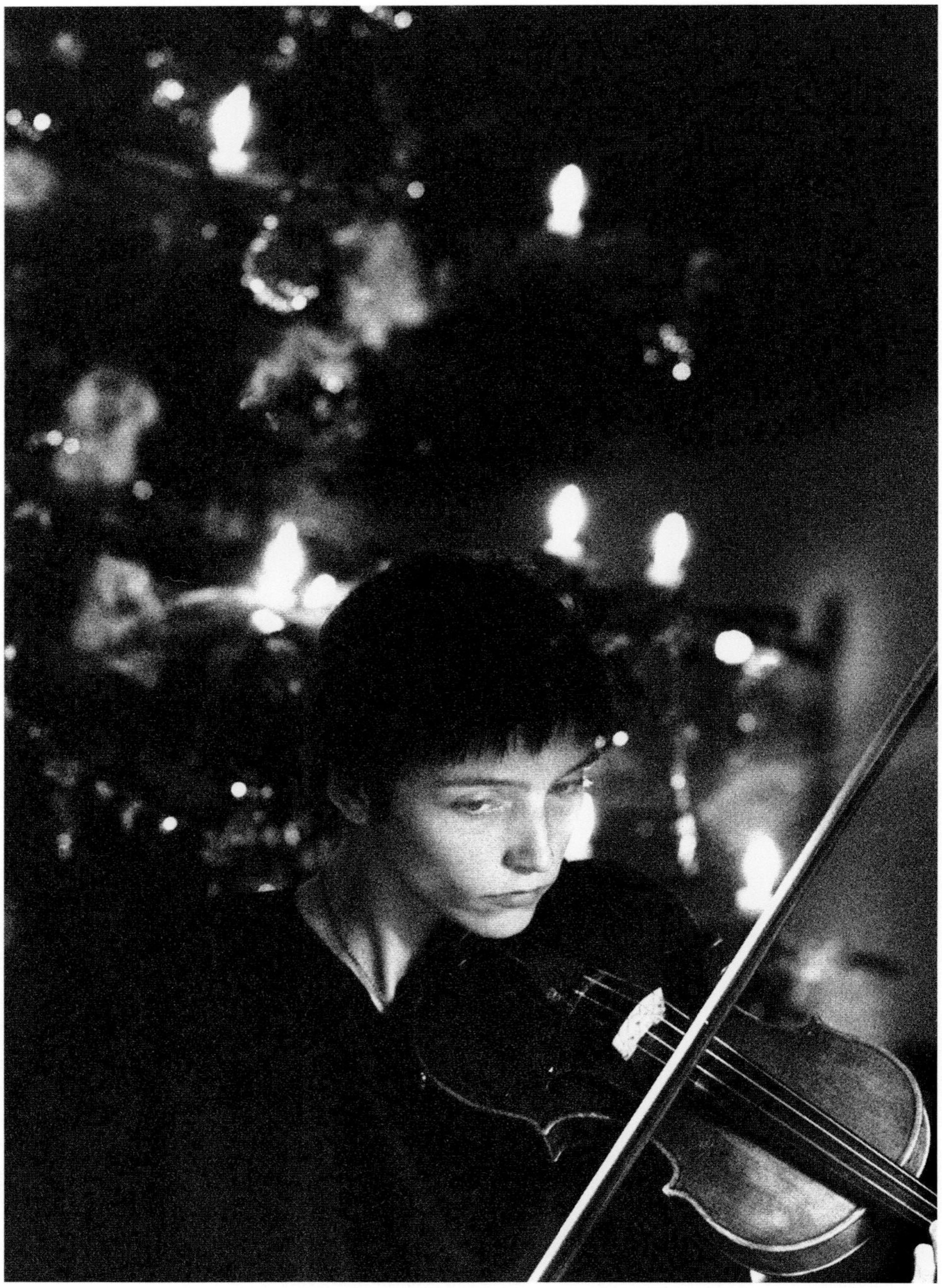

Hotel Chesa Guardalej, Champfèr

Park Hotels Waldhaus, Flims

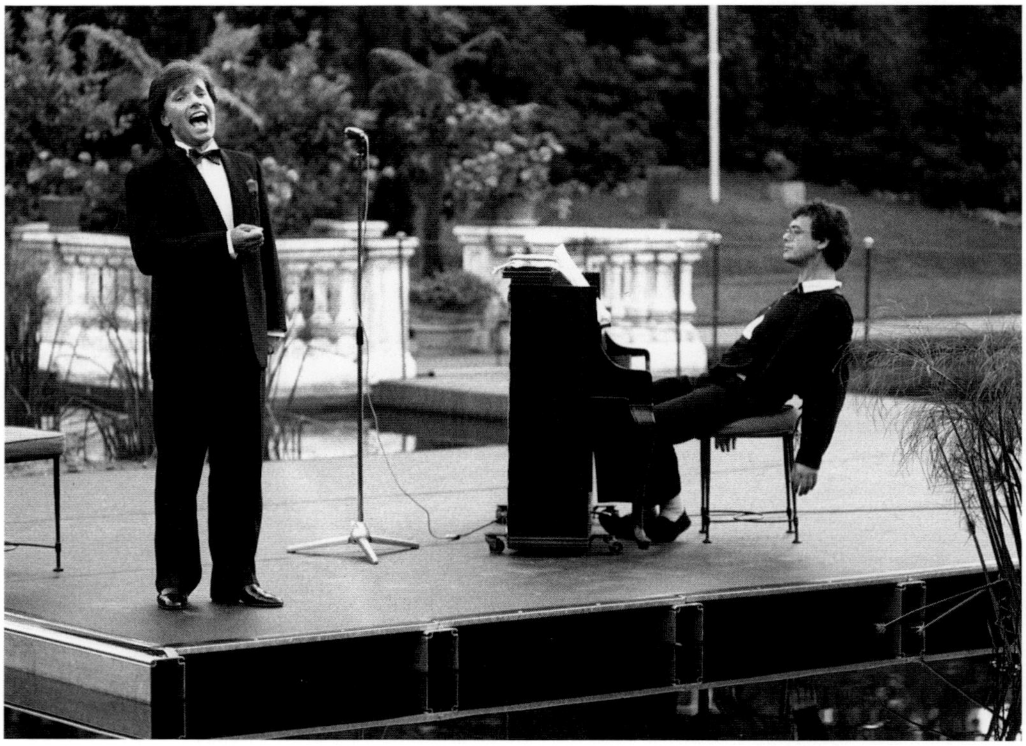

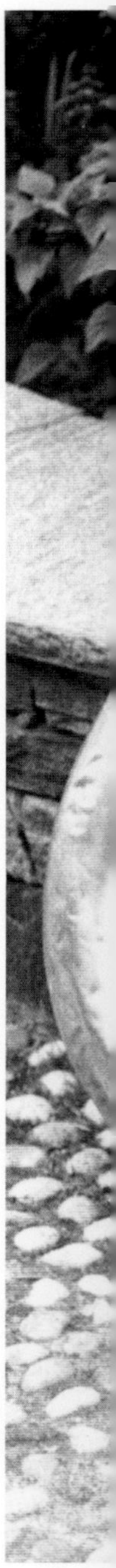

Relais & Châteaux Hôtel Giardino, Ascona

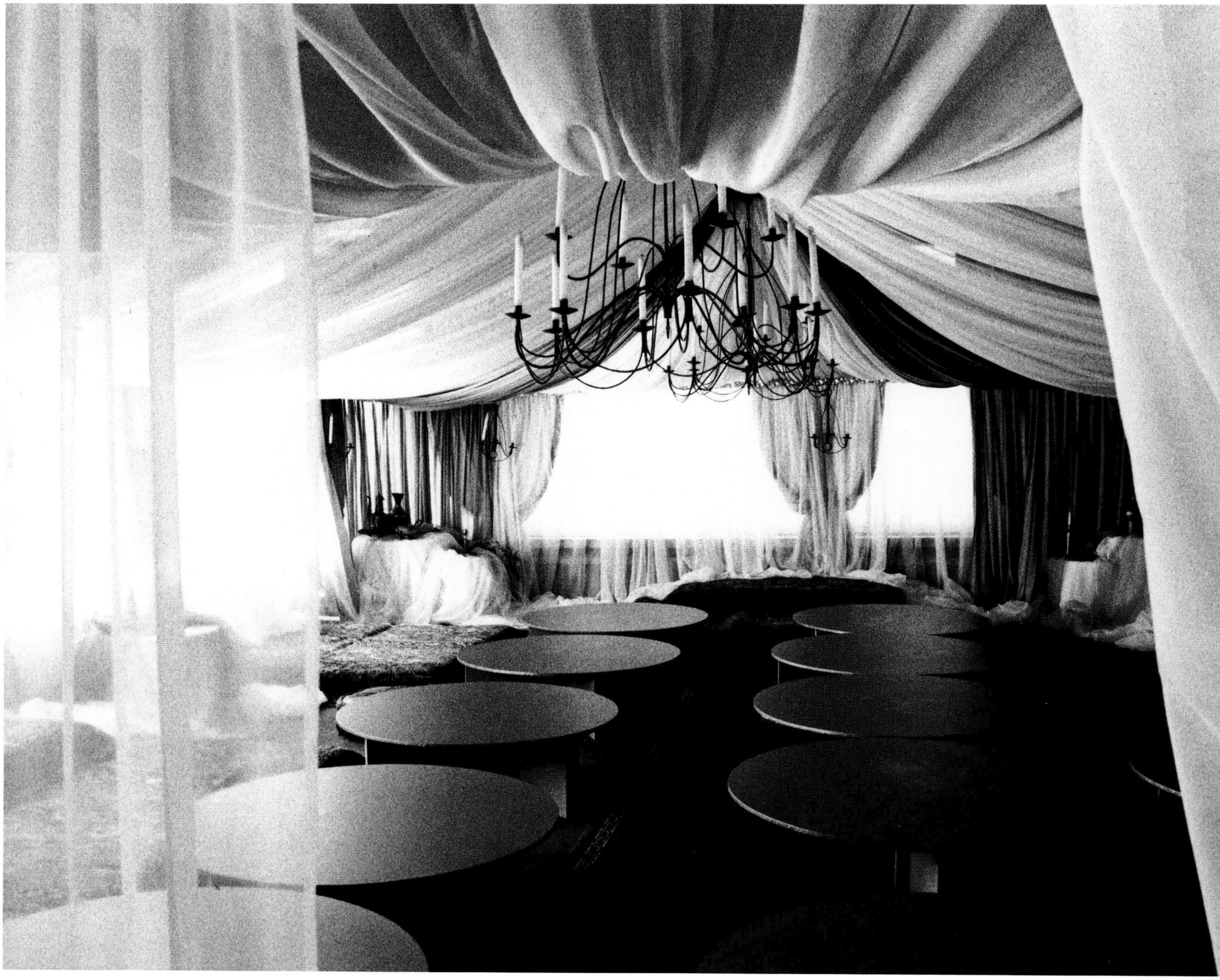

Hotel Eden, Arosa

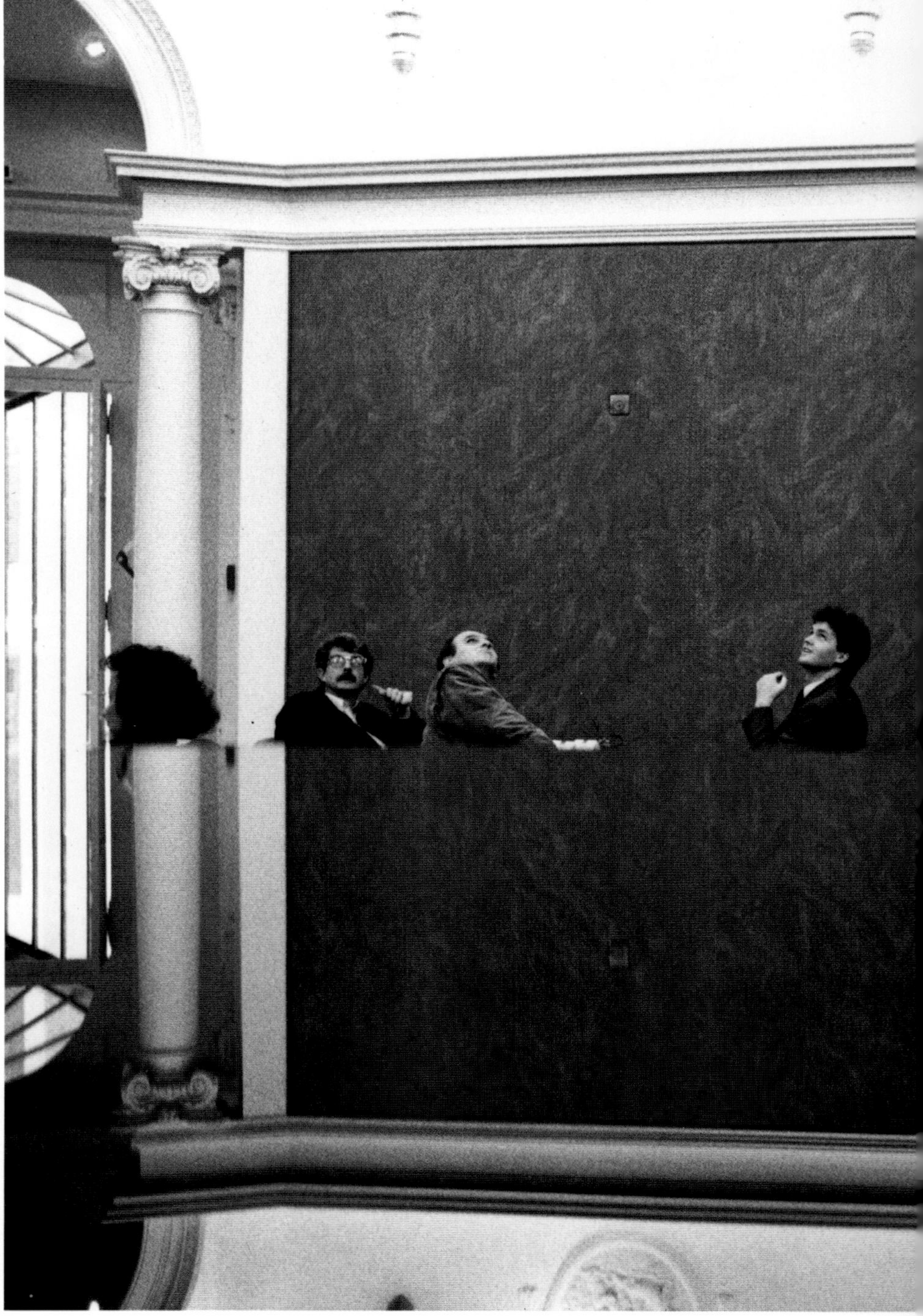

Grand Hôtel des Bains, Yverdon-les-Bains

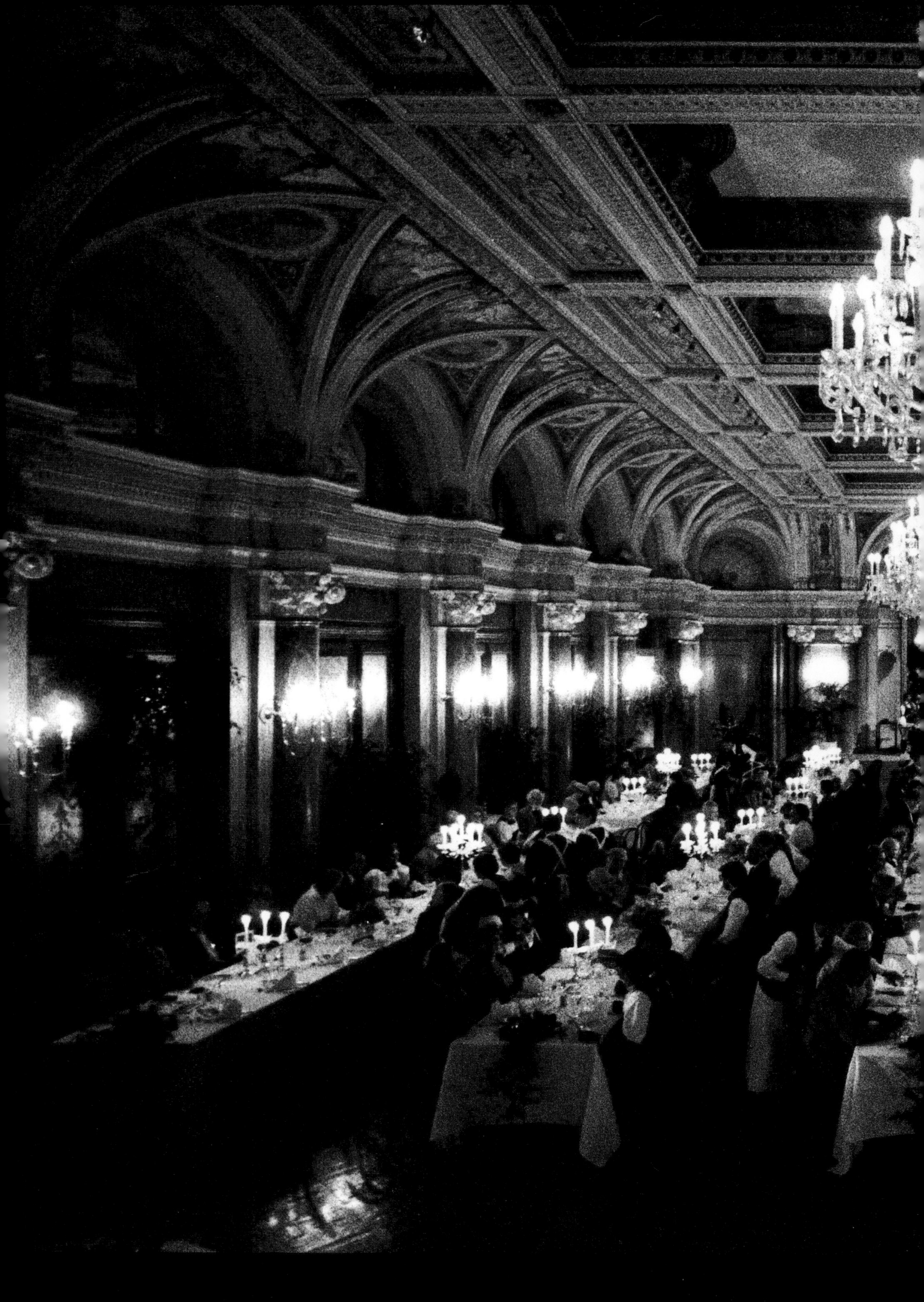

Grand Hotel Victoria-Jungfrau, Interlaken

Hotel Chasa Capòl, Santa Maria

Gasthof Hirschen am See, Meilen

Die 18 Ferienhotels
The 18 Resort Hotels

Name: Hotel Bristol
Adresse: 3954 Leukerbad
Gastgeber: Marie-Therese Loretan
Manfred Loretan
Anzahl Mitarbeiter: 68
Telefon: 027/61 18 33
Telefax: 027/61 36 87
Saison: Weihnachten – anfangs November
Kategorie: ***** SHV
Kategorie in Worten: Badehotel mit einer Spur Luxus
Anzahl Zimmer, ev. Hinweis auf Suiten: 78 Zimmer
Infrastruktur: Eigene Thermalquelle mit Hallen- und Freiluftschwimmbad, Schönheitsfarm Isabelle, Therapiezentrum, Coiffure, Sauna, Solarium; Hotelrestaurant, Carnotzet mit Walliser Spezialitäten, Garten- und Terrassenrestaurant.
Besonderes: Hier entstand die Idee zum vorliegenden Buch. Die Liebenswürdigkeit, mit der Marie-Therese Loretan ihren Gästen und Mitarbeitern begegnet, hat uns tief beeindruckt.

Name: Hotel Bristol
Address: 3954 Leukerbad
Hosts: Marie-Therese Loretan
Manfred Loretan
Number of staff: 68
Telephone: 027/61 18 33
Telefax: 027/61 36 87
Season: Christmas to early November
Category: ***** SHV
Category in words: Spa hotel with a dash of luxury
Number of rooms: 78 rooms
Infrastructure: Hotel-owned thermal spring with indoor and outdoor swimming pools, Isabelle beauty farm, therapy centre, hairdresser, sauna, solarium; hotel restaurant, carnotzet with Valaisan specialities, garden and terrace restaurant.
Special features: It was here that the idea of this book was born. The charm Marie-Therese Loretan displays in her dealings with guests and hotel employees deeply impressed us.

Name: Hotel Rebstock
Adresse: 6006 Luzern
Gastgeberin: Claudia Moser
Anzahl Mitarbeiter: 50
Telefon: 041/51 35 81
Telefax: 041/51 39 17
Saison: ganzes Jahr geöffnet
Kategorie: **** SHV
Kategorie in Worten: Erstklasshotel
Anzahl Zimmer, ev. Hinweis auf Suiten: 27 Zimmer, keine Suiten
Infrastruktur: Alle Zimmer mit TV-Video, Radio, Telefon, Bad/Dusche, WC, Lift, 2 Restaurants, Garten, Terrasse, Säli, Garagen und Parkplätze (kostenpflichtig)
Besonderes: Jedes Zimmer ist individuell eingerichtet. Durchgehend warme Küche aus der grossen Karte von 11.00–24.00 Uhr. Weinspezialitäten, grosses Frühstücksbuffet, vielfältige Spezialitätenwochen (Wild, Tartufi, internationale Wochen, Zwetschgen, Kirschen etc.) Das einzige Stadtferienhotel in diesem Buch, geprägt von seiner dynamischen und charmanten Gastgeberin.

Name: Hotel Rebstock
Address: 6006 Lucerne
Host: Claudia Moser
Number of staff: 50
Telephone: 041/51 35 81
Telefax: 041/51 39 17
Season: Open all the year
Category: **** SHV
Category in words: First-class hotel
Number of rooms, with any suites: 27 rooms, no suites
Infrastructure: All rooms with TV-video, radio, telephone, bath/shower, WC, lift, 2 restaurants, garden, terrace, banquet room, garages and parking spaces (extra charge).
Special features: Every room is individually furnished. Hot meals from a large menu from 11 am to 12 pm, special wines, varied breakfast buffet, a wide range of speciality weeks (game, tartufi, international cuisine, plums, cherries, etc.). The only city holiday hotel in this book, bearing the stamp of its dynamic and charming host.

Name: Märchenhotel Bellevue
Adresse: 8784 Braunwald
Gastgeber: Martin und Lydia Vogel-Curty
Anzahl Mitarbeiter: 35
Telefon: 058/84 38 43
Telefax: 058/84 22 74
Saison: Weihnachten bis Ostern/ Anfang Juni bis Ende Oktober
Kategorie: **** SHV
Kategorie in Worten: Das Märchenhotel zum Anfassen
Anzahl Zimmer: 60
Infrastruktur: Ferienhotel im autofreien Braunwald mit eigenem Hallenbad, betreutem Kindergarten und vielen Aufenthaltsräumen.
Besonderes: Der Gastgeber höchstpersönlich erzählt jeden Abend allen Kindern der Hotelgäste selbst ausgedachte Märchen – unterdessen geniessen Mama und Papa den Kaffee in der Hotelbar.

Name: Märchenhotel Bellevue
Address: 8784 Braunwald
Hosts: Martin and Lydia Vogel-Curty
Number of staff: 35
Telephone: 058/84 38 43
Telefax: 058/84 22 74
Season: Christmas to Easter/Beginning of June to end of October
Categorie: **** SHV
Categorie in words: The fairy-story hotel come true
Number of rooms: 60 rooms
Infrastructure: Resort hotel in traffic-free Braunwald with its own indoor swimming pool, supervised kindergarten and numbers of guest lounges.
Special features: The host himself tells the children of hotel guests fairy stories of his own invention every evening, while mummy and daddy enjoy a coffee in the hotel bar.

Name:	**Hôtel le Vieux Manoir au Lac**
Adresse:	3280 Murten/Meyriez
Gastgeber:	Elisabeth & Erich Thomas
Besitzerin:	Annelise Leu
Anzahl Mitarbeiter:	50
Telefon:	037/71 12 83
Telefax:	037/71 31 88
Saison:	Ende Februar bis anfangs Dezember
Kategorie:	**** SHV

Kategorie in Worten: Relais & Châteaux Hotel direkt am See umgeben von prächtigen Bäumen

Anzahl Zimmer, ev. Hinweis auf Suiten: 20 Zimmer, 2 Turmsuiten

Infrastruktur: Eigener Bootssteg, Privathafen, Sandstrand; Gourmet Restaurant mit Seeterrasse.

Besonderes: Das herrschaftliche, ja fast schlossartige Haus wurde kürzlich mit Liebe und Geschmack neu renoviert. Jedes Zimmer ist individuell eingerichtet. Hier sind Kulinarik und Romantik wunderbar vereint.

Name:	**Hôtel Le Vieux Manoir au Lac**
Address:	3280 Morat/Meyriez
Hosts:	Elisabeth & Erich Thomas
Proprietor:	Annelise Leu
Number of staff:	50
Telephone:	037/71 12 83
Telefax:	037/71 31 88
Season:	End of February to early December
Category:	**** SHV

Category in words: Relais & Châteaux hotel by the lakeside, surrounded by splendid trees

Number of rooms, with any suites: 20 rooms, 2 tower suites

Infrastructure: Private boat landing-stage and harbour, sandy beach; gourmet restaurant with lake terrace.

Special features: The stately, castle-like house was recently renovated with discernment and love. Every room is individually appointed. Culinary and romantic qualities are here wonderfully blended.

Name:	**Theater Hotel Chasa Capòl**
Adresse:	7536 Santa Maria/GR
Gastgeber:	Familie E.T.A. Schweizer
Anzahl Mitarbeiter:	6 Familienmitglieder und 6 weitere Mitarbeiter
Telefon:	082/8 57 28
Saison:	ganzes Jahr geöffnet
Kategorie in Worten:	romantisches Hotel der Sonderklasse

Anzahl Zimmer, ev. Hinweis auf Suiten: 13 Zimmer, 1 Suite im Haupthaus; 7 Zimmer mit fl. Wasser (ohne Komfort) in der Dépendance «Villetta Capolina»

Infrastruktur: Gourmet-Restaurant im Rittersaal und in der Stüva; Garten-Restaurant; Hotelpark mit Boccia und Schwimmbad (28 °C); Bar Bohème im ehemaligen Malefiz-Kerker; Bar Marco Polo, Treffpunkt am Cheminée; Weinkellerei mit Südtiroler Eigenbauweinen; hauseigenes Theater; Hauskapelle und Museum; Butia sur Traschenda (Boutique); Kunstgalerie.

Besonderes: «Jeder Raum ein Geschichten-Zimmer mit Theater, Musik und Lichterschimmer, mit Lieblingsspeisen und gutem Wein und freundlichen Menschen... Schon bald ist man versucht zu denken: Es muss so sein!» B. S. über Chasa Capòl

Name:	**Theater Hotel Chasa Capòl**
Address:	7536 Santa Maria/Grisons
Hosts:	E.T.A. Schweizer and family
Number of staff:	6 members of the family and 6 others
Telephone:	082/8 57 28
Season:	Open all the year
Category in words:	Romantic hotel in a special class

Number of rooms, with any suites: 13 rooms, 1 suite in the main building; 7 rooms with running water (but simply appointed) in the annexe, Villetta Capolina

Infrastructure: Gourmet restaurant in the great hall and in the Stüva; garden restaurant; hotel park with boccia and swimming pool (28 °C); Bohème Bar in the former malefactors' prison: Marco Polo Bar, with open fireplace; wine cellars with hotel-grown South Tyrolean wines; hotel theatre; house chapel and museum; Butia sur Traschenda (boutique); art gallery.

Special features: "Every room a historical scene, with theatre, music and lights between, with favourite dishes and excellent wine, and friendly people... You can't help thinking, this is just the right line!" B.S. on Chasa Capòl.

Name:	**Hotel Chesa Guardalej**
Adresse:	7512 St. Moritz/Champfèr
Gastgeber:	Frank H. und Helene Wolf
Saison:	Sommer und Winter
Anzahl Mitarbeiter:	90–120
Telefon:	082/2 31 21
Telefax:	082/3 23 73
Kategorie:	**** SHV

Kategorie in Worten: Das besondere Viersternhotel mit Ambiente

Anzahl Zimmer, ev. Hinweis auf Suiten: 114 Zimmer, 2 Suiten

Infrastruktur: Hallenschwimmbad, Saunas, Solarium, Whirl Pool, Massage, «Folterkammer», Squashhalle, Ping-Pong, Billard, Spielhölle, Boutique, 3 Restaurants, Bar/Kaminhalle, Konferenzräume, Kinderdîners mit Betreuung, hoteleigenes Parkhaus.

Besonderes: Trotz der Grösse des Hotels fühlt man sich hier wie in einem privaten Engadiner Haus zu Gast. Die fachkundigen und fröhlichen Mitarbeiter, das fazettenreiche Freizeitangebot und kulinarische Höhenflüge lassen einen Besuch unvergesslich werden.

Name:	**Hotel Chesa Gurdalej**
Address:	7512 St. Moritz/Champfèr
Hosts:	Frank H. and Helene Wolf
Season:	Summer and winter
Number of staff:	90–120
Telephone:	082/2 31 21
Telefax:	082/3 23 73
Categorie:	**** SHV

Category in words: The special four-star hotel with ambiente

Number of rooms, with any suites: 114 rooms, 2 suites

Infrastructure: Indoor swimming pool, saunas, solarium, whirlpool, massage, "torture chamber", squash court, table tennis, billiards, gambling den, three restaurants, bar/fireside hall, conference rooms, children's dinners with attendants, own indoor car park.

Special features: In spite of the size of the hotel the guest feels like a private visitor to an Engadine house. The cheerful, well-trained staff, the varied range of pastimes and the culinary flights suffice to make a stay here unforgettable.

Name: **Hotel Europe**

Adresse: Promenadengasse 63, 7270 Davos Platz

Gastgeber: Erich Schmid

Anzahl Mitarbeiter: 90

Telefon: 081/43 59 21
Telefax: 081/43 13 93

Kategorie: **** SHV

Kategorie in Worten: Ferienhotel am Puls von Davos

Anzahl Zimmer, ev. Hinweis auf Suiten: 6 Suiten, 40 Doppelzimmer, 18 Einzelzimmer, 40 Appartements in der Résidence

Infrastruktur: Scala – Restaurant Café; Zauberberg – China Restaurant; Au Premier – Restaurant français; Tonic – Piano Bar; Cabanna Club – Disco; Cava Grischa – Kellerlokal mit Live-Musik; Fitness- und Beautycenter, Hallenschwimmbad; Sauna, Billard Club; Tennisplatz; Garten mit Liegewiese; Kinderspielplatz; Coiffeur; Einstellgarage; Ladenstrasse.

Besonderes: Spezial-Arrangements wie Schönheits- und Fitnesswochen, Lauf- und Plauschwoche, Mountain Bike-Woche oder Billard-Ferienwoche. Vor kurzem völlig neu gestaltet zu einem eigenwilligen Ferienhotel mit vielen ausgefallenen Ideen.

Name: **Hotel Europe**

Address: Promenadengasse 63, 7270 Davos Platz

Host: Erich Schmid

Number of staff: 90

Telephone: 081/43 59 21
Telefax: 081/43 13 93

Category: **** SHV

Category in words: Resort hotel close to the pulsebeat of Davos

Number of rooms, with any suites: 6 suites, 40 twin-bedded rooms, 18 single rooms, 40 apartments in the Résidence

Infrastructure: Scala, restaurant café; Zauberberg, Chinese restaurant; Au Premier, French restaurant; Tonic piano bar; Cabanna Club disco; Cava Grischa cellar with live music; fitness and beauty centre; indoor swimming pool; sauna, billiard club; tennis court; garden with sunbathing lawn; children's playground; hairdresser; parking garage; shopping mall.

Special features: Special arrangements such as beauty and fitness weeks, mountain bike weeks and billiard holiday weeks. Recently redesigned as an original holiday hotel with lots of unusual ideas.

Name: **Hotel Furkablick**

Adresse: 6491 Realp

Gastgeber: Marc Hostettler

Anzahl Mitarbeiter: 8

Telefon: 044/6 72 97, wenn keine Antwort: 038/24 53 23

Saison: während den Sommermonaten

Kategorie: Passhotel, erbaut während der Jahrhundertwende (2430 m.ü.M.)

Anzahl Zimmer, ev. Hinweis auf Suiten: 20

Infrastruktur: alle Zimmer ohne fliessendes Wasser, Etagenduschen, grosser Aufenthaltsraum, Speisesaal, Restaurant

Besonderes: Das «Kulturlaboratorium» Furk'art, das Originalmobiliar, nicht zuletzt das eben renovierte Restaurant O.M.A. und die Passwildnis lassen einen Besuch zu einem in jeder Hinsicht aussergewöhnlichen Hotelerlebnis werden.

Name: **Hotel Furkablick**

Address: 6491 Realp

Host: Marc Hostettler

Number off staff: 8

Telephone: 044/6 72 97, if unanswered 038/24 53 23

Season: Summer months

Category: Pass hotel built at the turn of the century (8000 ft.)

Number of rooms, with any suites: 20 rooms

Infrastructure: No running water in the rooms, one shower on each floor, large lounge, dining room, restaurant.

Special features: The Furk'art "culture laboratory", the original furnishings, the recently renovated O.M.A. restaurant and the wilderness of the pass itself make a visit a thoroughly extraordinary hotel experience.

Name: **Hôtel de la Gare**

Adresse: 2725 Le Noirmont

Gastgeber: Andrea & Georges Wenger

Anzahl Mitarbeiter: 20

Telefon: 039/53 11 10
Telefax: 039/53 10 59

Kategorie: **** SHV

Kategorie in Worten: Luxuriöser Gasthof

Saison: Ganzes Jahr geöffnet

Anzahl Zimmer, ev. Hinweis auf Suiten: 1 Doppelzimmer, 2 Mini-Suiten

Infrastruktur: Die drei Zimmer sind für höchste Ansprüche ausgestattet. Gourmet-Restaurant; Sonnenterrasse, Garten.

Besonderes: Der gute Ruf von Georges Wengers Küche ist weit über die Schweizer Grenzen hinaus bekannt. Sein Restaurant gehört zu den fünfzig besten in der Schweiz.

Name: **Hôtel de la Gare**

Address: 2725 Le Noirmont

Hosts: Andrea & Georges Wenger

Number of staff: 20

Telephone: 039/53 11 10
Telefax: 039/53 10 59

Category: **** SHV

Category in words: Luxurious guesthouse

Season: Open all the year

Number of rooms, with any suites: 1 twin-bedded room, 2 mini-suites

Infrastructure: The three rooms are designed to satisfy highest requirements. Gourmet restaurant; sun terrace, garden.

Special features: The good reputation of Georges Wenger's cuisine has spread far beyond Swiss frontiers. His restaurant ranks among the fifty best in Switzerland.

Name:	**Relais & Châteaux Hôtel Giardino**
Adresse:	6612 Ascona
Gastgeber:	Hans C. Leu
Anzahl Mitarbeiter:	120
Telefon:	093/35 01 01
Telefax:	093/36 10 94
Saison:	Mitte März bis Mitte November
Kategorie:	***** SHV

Kategorie in Worten: Elegantes südliches Landhaus

Anzahl Zimmer, ev. Hinweis auf Suiten: 54 Doppelzimmer, 18 Suiten

Infrastruktur: Restaurant Giardino – französische Küche; Restaurant Aphrodite – italienische Küche; Pool Café; «Vanity Bellezza» – Schönheits-Center; 48 rosarote Velos und ein rosaroter Oldtimer Bus von Hans C. Leu offeriert für Ausflüge.

Besonderes: Sein Name hält, was er verspricht: Der Garten des «Giardino» ist rund ums Jahr eine Pracht. Das «Teatro Giardino» unterhält die Gäste mit Ballett, Musical, Schauspiel oder Jazz – die Bühne: auf dem Seerosenteich.

Name:	**Relais & Châteaux Hôtel Giardino**
Address:	6612 Ascona
Host:	Hans C. Leu
Number of staff:	120
Telephone:	093/35 01 01
Telefax:	093/36 10 94
Season:	Mid-March to mid–November
Category:	***** SHV
Category in words:	Stylish southern country house

Number of rooms: 54 twin-bedded rooms, 18 suites

Infrastructure: Giardino Restaurant, French – cuisine; Aphrodite Restaurant – Italian cuisine; Pool Café; "Vanity Bellezza" – beauty centre; 48 pink bicycles and a pink old-timer bus, offered by Hans C. Leu for outings.

Special features: The Giardino lives up to its name – the garden is a splendid sight all the year round. The Teatro Giardino entertains guests with ballet, musicals, plays or jazz, the stage is on the waterlily pond.

Name:	**Grand Hôtel des Bains**
Adresse:	1400 Yverdon-les-Bains
Gastgeber:	Claude Giauque
Anzahl Mitarbeiter:	60
Telefon:	024/21 70 21
Telefax:	024/21 21 90
Saison:	Ganzes Jahr geöffnet
Kategorie:	**** SHV

Kategorie in Worten: Ein Badehotel aus drei Epochen

Anzahl Zimmer, ev. Hinweis auf Suiten: 114 Zimmer, 10 Suiten

Infrastruktur: Gourmetrestaurant «Le Pavillon»; Hotelrestaurant «La Belle Epoque»; Terassencafé; Piano Bar «La Rotonde»; Seminarräume; eigenes Freiluftthermalbad (34 °C); direkter Zugang zum Thermalcenter Yverdon-les-Bains; Schönheits- und Fitness-Center (Sauna, Dampfbad, Solarium); Coiffeur und Kurabteilung.

Besonderes: 1989 eröffnete das Grand Hôtel des Bains seine Türen. Das Bade- und Kurhotel vereint harmonisch drei Bauepochen: Den Schlosstrakt aus dem Jahr 1734, den Kuppelbau mit Ballsaal aus dem Jahr 1896 und einen modernen Rundbau, der das 20. Jahrhundert repräsentiert.

Name:	**Grand Hôtel des Bains**
Address:	1400 Yverdon-les-Bains
Host:	Claude Giauque
Number of staff:	60
Telephone:	024/21 70 21
Telefax:	024/21 21 90
Season:	Open all the year
Category:	**** SHV
Category in words:	A spa hotel dating from three epochs

Number of rooms, with any suites: 114 rooms, 10 suites

Infrastructure: Le Pavillon gourmet restaurant; La Belle Epoque hotel restaurant; terrace café; La Rotonde piano bar; conference rooms; hotel-owned open-air thermal swimming pool (34°C); direct access to Yverdon-les-Bains balneological centre; beauty and fitness centre (sauna, steam bath, solarium); hairdresser and therapy department.

Special features: The Grand Hôtel des Bains opened in 1989. A hotel with its own spa facilities, it is a harmonious blend of architecture from three periods: the castle wing from 1734, the cupola with ballroom from 1896, and a modern rotunda representing the twentieth century.

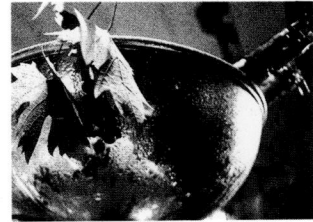

Name:	**Gasthof Hirschen am See**
Adresse:	8706 Meilen
Gastgeber:	Marissa und Bruno Liniger
Anzahl Mitarbeiter:	38
Telefon:	01/923 65 51
Telefax:	01/923 34 53
Saison:	Ganzes Jahr geöffnet
Kategorie:	*** SHV

Kategorie in Worten: Gasthof an glücklicher Lage...

Anzahl Zimmer, ev. Hinweis auf Suiten: 16 Zimmer

Infrastruktur: Restaurant mit grosser Seeterrasse, Taverne, Bar.

Besonderes: Bereits 1605 wurde für den Gasthof zum Hirschen ein Tavernenrecht ausgegeben. Seither ist es immer eine Gaststätte geblieben, teilweise auch als Hauptquartier der einheimischen Kavalleristen. Anlässlich der letzten Um- und Ausbauten war es oberstes Ziel, den Gästen den Charme dieses über 300jährigen Hauses zu erhalten – und gleichzeitig den heutigen Ansprüchen gerecht zu werden.

Name:	**Gasthof Hirschen am See**
Address:	8706 Meilen
Hosts:	Marissa and Bruno Liniger
Number of staff:	38
Telephone:	01/923 65 51
Telefax:	01/923 34 53
Season:	Open all the year
Category:	*** SHV
Category in words:	An inn in a happy situation…

Number of rooms, with any suites: 16 rooms

Infrastructure: Restaurant with large lake terrace, tavern, bar.

Special features: A tavern charter was granted to the Gasthof zum Hirschen as far back as 1605. Since then it has remained an inn, at times being the headquarters of the local cavalry. When it was last renovated and extended, the goal was to satisfy modern requirements while preserving for its guests all the charm of a house over 300 years old.

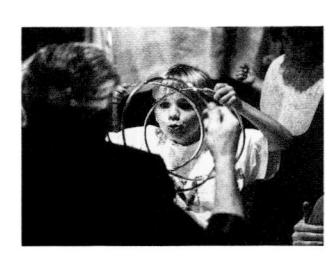

Name:	**Hotel Lago di Lugano**
Adresse:	6816 Bissone
Gastgeber:	Uschi und Alf Omischl-Kobi
Anzahl Mitarbeiter:	Sommer bis 90, Winter bis 30
Telefon:	091/68 85 91
Telefax:	091/68 61 81
Saison:	Mitte März bis anfangs Januar
Kategorie:	**** SHV

Kategorie in Worten: Grosszügiges Familienferienhotel mitten in Parkanlage, direkt am Luganersee

Anzahl Zimmer, ev. Hinweis auf Suiten: 70 Zimmer, 10 Juniorsuiten, 9 Suiten

Infrastruktur: Hotelrestaurant «Millefiori» mit Kinderecke, Rôtisserie Il Roseto und Ristorante Al Porto direkt am See; betreuter Kindergarten, Spielzimmer, Videothek, Bibliothek, Sauna, Solarium; im Freien: geheiztes Schwimmbad, Gartenschach, Tischtennis, Bocciabahn, Liegewiese, Bootshafen.

Besonderes: Die kleinen Gäste fühlen sich hier ebenso wohl wie Mama und Papa. Von der Baby-Checkliste, über die professionelle Kindergärtnerin bis zu den von Alf Omischl begleiteten Ausflügen für 10- bis 16jährige gibt es hier alles, was ein Kinderherz begehrt.

Name:	**Hotel Lago di Lugano**
Address:	6816 Bissone
Hosts:	Uschi and Alf Omischl-Kobi
Number of staff:	Up to 90 in summer, up to 30 in winter
Telephone:	091/68 85 91
Telefax:	091/68 61 81
Season:	Mid-March to early January
Category:	**** SHV

Category in words: Spacious family holiday hotel in a park on the shore of the Lake of Lugano

Number of rooms, with any suites: 70 rooms, 10 junior suites, 9 suites

Infrastructure: Millefiori Restaurant with children's corner, Il Roseto rôtisserie and Ristorante Al Porto by the lake; supervised kindergarten, playroom, videothèque, library, sauna, solarium; outdoors: heated swimming pool, garden chess, table tennis, boccia court, sunbathing lawn, boat harbour.

Special features: Small guests feel just as much at home here as their mummies and daddies. This is a place where children's dreams come true; there is everything from a baby check list to a professional kindergarten teacher and excursions for children from ten to sixteen escorted by Alf Omischl himself.

Name:	**Hotel Haus Paradies**
Adresse:	7551 Ftan
Gastgeber:	Roland und Brigitte Jöhri
Anzahl Mitarbeiter:	40
Telefon:	084/9 13 25
Telefax:	084/9 17 74
Saison:	Winter: vor Weihnachten bis Ostern. Sommer: Anfangs Juni bis Ende Oktober
Kategorie:	**** SHV

Kategorie in Worten: Sehr ruhig gelegenes Relais & Châteaux-Hotel und Relais Gourmand

Anzahl Zimmer, ev. Hinweis auf Suiten: 13 Zimmer, 8 Suiten

Infrastruktur: Alle Zimmer sind gegen Süden gerichtet, Sauna, Solarium und Physiotherapie, 2 Sandtennisplätze ganz in der Nähe, Tiefgarage (pro Zimmer ein Platz).

Besonderes: Das Hotel liegt auf einem Sonnenplateau mit fantastischer Aussicht und erweckt den Eindruck eines gepflegten Privathauses. Eine erstklassige Bibliothek sowie das Kamin- und Bridgezimmer stehen als Aufenthaltsräume bereit. Ein mit vielen Raritäten bestücktes Alpinum und der vom Hausherrn gehegte Kräutergarten sind zwei weitere Sehenswürdigkeiten.

Name:	**Hotel Haus Paradies**
Address:	7551 Ftan
Hosts:	Roland and Brigitte Jöhri
Number of staff:	40
Telephone:	084/9 13 25
Telefax:	084/9 17 74
Season:	Winter: Before Christmas to Easter. Summer: Beginning of June to end of October
Category:	**** SHV

Category in words: Relais & Châteaux hotel in a very quiet situation and Relais Gourmand

Number of rooms, with any suites: 13 rooms, 8 suites

Infrastructure: All rooms are south-facing; sauna, solarium and physiotherapy; 2 clay tennis courts near by, underground car park (one parking space per room).

Special features: The hotel lies on a sunny plateau with a fantastic view and gives the impression of a well-kept private house. There is a first-class library and a bridge room with an open fireplace. An Alpine garden with many rare plants and a herb garden tended by the hotel manager himself are also worth seeing.

Name:	**Park Hotels Waldhaus**
Adresse:	7018 Flims
Gastgeber:	Josef Müller
Anzahl Mitarbeiter:	150
Telefon:	081/39 01 81
Telefax:	081/39 28 04
Saison:	Ende Mai bis Ende Oktober Mitte Dezember bis Mitte April
Kategorie:	***** SHV

Kategorie in Worten: Hotelanlage im grössten Privatpark der Schweiz

Anzahl Zimmer, ev. Hinweis auf Suiten: 160 Zimmer, 30 Junior-Suiten und Suiten, 1 Jugendstilsuite, 1 Kunstsuite, 20 Appartements

Infrastruktur: Hotelspeisesäle: Panorama-Restaurant, Rotonde, Piccolo, Waldhaussaal, *Jugendstilsaal für Fest- und Galaanlässe,* Spezialitätenrestaurant La Cena, Garten- und Terassenrestaurant; Bar-Dancing Chadafö, Party-Lokal Il Tschalèr, Waldhaus Tagesbar, Halle Waldhaus und Halle Pavillon, Bridge Room, TV Room, Tennis (9 Aussen- und 2 Hallenplätze), Hallen- und Gartenbad mit Sauna, Solarium, Massage; Hair & Beauty Salon; Golftrainingsanlage im Park.

Besonderes: Ferienhotel im Pavillonsystem mit zwei vollständig ausgestatteten Seminar- und Kommunikationszentren. Der Jugendstil-Festsaal steht unter Denkmalschutz und lässt das Herz jedes Fin-de-siècle-Begeisterten höher schlagen. Mit der Kunstgalerie und ihren wechselnden Ausstellungen, Giovanni Giacomettis Flimser Panorama und dem Opern Essttheater «La Cena è pronta» leistet das Haus Beiträge zu Kunst und Kultur. Kurse mit der international bekannten amerikanischen PBI-Tennisschule (Peter Burwash International).

Name:	**Park Hotels Waldhaus**
Address:	7018 Flims
Host:	Josef Müller
Number of staff:	150
Telephone:	081/39 01 81
Telefax:	081/39 28 04
Season:	End of May to end of October Mid-December to mid-April
Category:	***** SHV

Category in words: Hotel estate situated in Switzerland's largest private park

Number of rooms, with any suites: 160 rooms, 30 junior suites and suites, 1 Art Nouveau suite, 1 art suite, 20 apartments

Infrastructure: Hotel dining rooms: Panorama Restaurant, Rotonde, Piccolo, Waldhaussaal, *Art Nouveau hall for banquets and galas,* La Cena speciality restaurant, garden and terrace restaurant, Chadafö bar and dance floor, Il Tschalèr party room, Waldhaus day bar, Waldhaus hall and Pavilion hall, bridge room, TV room, tennis (9 outdoor and 2 indoor courts), indoor and garden swimming pool with sauna, solarium, massage; hair and beauty salon; golf training facility in the park.

Special features: Resort hotel in the pavilion system with two fully equipped seminar and communications centres. The Art Nouveau banquet hall is classified as a historic monument and is a delight for all lovers of a *fin-de-siècle* ambiance. The hotel makes its contribution to art and culture with the changing exhibitions in its art gallery, with Giovanni Giacometti's Panorama of Flims, and with dining-room operas ("La cena è pronta"). Tennis courses can be taken with the internationally reputed PBI (Peter Burwash International) tennis school.

Name:	**Hotel Principe Leopoldo**	
Adresse:	6900 Lugano – Via Montalbano 5	
Gastgeber:	Peter Gantenbein	
Anzahl Mitarbeiter:	68 zusammen mit Hotel Montalbano	
Telefon:	091/55 88 55	
Telefax:	091/54 25 38	
Saison:	Ganzes Jahr geöffnet	
Kategorie:	***** SHV	

Kategorie in Worten: Kleines Luxus-Hotel mit persönlichem Charme

Anzahl Zimmer, ev. Hinweis auf Suiten: 24 Junior-Suiten

Infrastruktur: Gastronomisches Restaurant, Piano Bar, Schwimmbad, Sauna, Solarium, Fitness-Raum, Whirlpool, Tennis, Indoor-Golf, Konferenz-, Tagungs- und Banketträumlichkeiten. Im Park des Principe Leopoldo steht das Hotel Montalbano mit weiteren 44 Juniorsuiten. Seine Gäste geniessen die Infrastruktur des Haupthauses. Hotel-Limousine-Service zum Flughafen Lugano/Agno, zum Bahnhof und ins Stadtzentrum.

Besonderes: Rundblick und Bau der Villa Principe Leopoldo sind fürstlich. So erstaunt es nicht, dass das prachtvolle Anwesen einst einem Hohenzollern-Prinzen gehörten. Das Haus wurde renoviert und zu einem kleinen, äusserst feinen Luxushotel umgewandelt.

Name:	**Hotel Principe Leopoldo**	
Address:	6900 Lugano, Via Montalbano 5	
Host:	Peter Gantenbein	
Number of staff:	68 with Hotel Montalbano	
Telephone:	091/55 88 55	
Telefax:	091/54 25 38	
Season:	Open all the year	
Category:	***** SHV	

Category in words: Small luxury hotel with personal charm

Number of rooms, with any suites: 24 junior suites

Infrastructure: Gastronomic restaurant, piano bar, swimming pool, sauna, solarium, fitness room, whirlpool, tennis, indoor golf, conference rooms and banquet halls. The Hotel Montalbano with 44 junior suites stands in the Principe Leopoldo Park. Its guests share the infrastructure of the main house. Hotel limousine service to Lugano/Agno airport, station and city centre.

Special features: The architecture and the panoramic view of the Villa Principe Leopoldo are in keeping with its princely name. It will surprise no one to learn that the magnificent estate once belonged to a Hohenzollern prince. The villa was renovated when it was converted into a small but very select luxury hotel.

Name:	**Grand Hotel Victoria-Jungfrau**	
Adresse:	3800 Interlaken	
Gastgeber:	Rosmarie und Emanuel Berger-Borer	
Anzahl Mitarbeiter:	im Sommer 240, im Winter 180	
Telefon:	036/21 21 71	
Telefax:	036/22 26 71	
Saison:	Zwischensaison: Januar bis März und 1.–20. Dezember Hochsaison: April bis November, Weihnachten, Neujahr	
Kategorie:	***** SHV	

Kategorie in Worten: Luxus Hotel

Anzahl Zimmer, ev. Hinweis auf Suiten: 177 Zimmer, 51 Junior-Suiten und Suiten (1-3 Zimmer)

Infrastruktur: Restaurants La Terrasse, Jungfraustube, Racket-Club; Intermezzo Bar, Victoria Bar; Hallenbad, Tenniscenter, ab Sommer 1992 exklusives Healt-Fitness- & Beauty Center; sechzehn Tagungs- und Banketträumlichkeiten für Anlässe von 4 bis 400 Personen.

Besonderes: Ohne zu übertreiben, darf man das Victoria-Jungfrau wohl das Flaggschiff der Schweizer Hotellerie nennen. 1865 öffnete es seine Türen. Heute, nach langen systematischen Erneuerungsarbeiten, bietet es Tradition der Jahrhundertwende und Hotelleistungen für höchste Ansprüche.

Name:	**Grand Hotel Victoria-Jungfrau**	
Address:	3800 Interlaken	
Hosts:	Rosmarie and Emanuel Berger-Borer	
Number of staff:	240 in summer, 180 in winter	
Telephone:	036/21 21 71	
Telefax:	036/22 26 71	
Season:	Intermediate: January to March and 1–20 December. High: April to November, Christmas, New Year	
Category:	***** SHV	
Category in words:	Luxury hotel	

Number of rooms, with any suites: 177 rooms, 51 junior suites and suites (1–3 rooms)

Infrastructure: Restaurant: La Terrasse, Jungfraustube and Racket-Club; Intermezzo Bar, Victoria Bar; indoor swimming pool, tennis centre, exclusive health, fitness and beauty centre from summer 1992; 16 conference rooms and banquet halls for 4 to 400 persons.

Special features: The Victoria-Jungfrau can claim, without exaggeration, to be the flagship of the Swiss hotel trade. It opened in 1865. Today, after long and systematic renovation, it offers the tradition of the turn of the century and a hotel service fulfilling the highest expectations.

Name:	**Hotel Eden**	
Adresse:	7050 Arosa	
Gastgeber:	Hitsch und Valerie Leu	
Anzahl Mitarbeiter:	45	
Telefon:	081/31 02 61	
Telefax:	081/31 40 66	
Saison:	anfangs Dezember bis Ostern	

Kategorie in Worten: Das extravagante Hotel für Ferien nach Lust und Laune

Anzahl Zimmer, ev. Hinweis auf Suiten: 79 Zimmer und 4 Suiten

Infrastruktur: Relax-Club mit Fitnessraum, Sauna, Dampfbad, Whirlpool, Solarium, Massagen und Physiotherapie, Aerobic- und Gymnastiklektionen; Speisesaal mit Frühstücksbuffet bis 12.00 Uhr, Weinrestaurant Barrick, kulinarische Gästetafeln, Erlebnishalle und Hotelbar mit Musikern des Jaylin's Club (Hotel Schweizerhof Bern); betreuter Kindergarten, Kinderesstisch; Disco Kitchen Club; Sonnenterrasse; Japanisches Restaurant «JUSHI»

Besonderes: Legendäre Feste, unkomplizierte, freundschaftliche Atmosphäre, Kulinarik inkl. Weinkultur auf hohem Niveau. Der kreative, eigenwillige Gastgeber zusammen mit seiner unkonventionellen Mitarbeiterpolitik machen das Hotel Eden zum Avantgarden.

Name:	**Hotel Eden**	
Address:	7050 Arosa	
Hosts:	Hitsch and Valerie Leu	
Number of staff:	45	
Telephone:	081/31 02 61	
Telefax:	081/31 40 66	
Season:	Beginning of December to Easter	

Category in words: The extravagant hotel for just the holidays you fancy

Number of rooms, with any suites: 79 rooms and four suites

Infrastructure: "Relax-Club" with fitness room, sauna, steam bath, whirlpool, solarium, massage and physiotherapy, aerobic and gymnastic lessons; dining room with breakfast buffet till 12 noon, Barrick wine restaurant, group feasts, entertainments hall and hotel bar with musicians of Jaylin's Club (Hotel Schweizerhof, Berne); supervised kindergarten, children's table at meals; Disco Kitchen Club; sun terrace; Japanese Restaurant "JUSHI".

Special features: Fabulous festivities, relaxed and friendly atmosphere, high culinary standards, select wines. The creative and original host and his unconventional staff policy make the Hotel Eden an avant-garde establishment.

Christoph Grünig. Geboren 1958 in Bern und aufgewachsen in Bern und Biel. Nach seiner Fotografenlehre in Thun arbeitete er während zwei Jahren als Freelancer bei verschiedenen Fotografen. 1982 entscheidet sich Christoph für die Selbständigkeit und eröffnet ein Studio für Werbefotografie in Biel. Sein Leitgedanke «Der Mensch im Mittelpunkt», der ihm zusammen mit der Kamera ständig begleitet, bleibt ihm nicht nur in Hotels treu, sondern auch in der Provence und in Andalusien, wo er zeitweise lebt.

Die Aufnahmen in diesem Buch entstanden mit einer Nikon F4 (Christoph Grünig versuchte es zuerst mit einer diskreten, kleinen Kamera; die «Hotelbewohner» reagierten überhaupt nicht.) und den Brennweiten 20 bis 35 sowie 105 Millimeter. Als Filmmaterial wurden die Filme Kodak T-Max 400 und 3200 verwendet.

Christoph über Christoph

Ich spaziere nach Hause. «Eigentlich könnte ich heute mit Stöh essen gehen… hm…vielleicht wieder einmal ins Paradiesli.» Zu Hause erwartet mich eine Nachricht auf dem Beantworter: «Hallo… hier Stöh… wir können doch zusammen essen gehen, ich schlage vor Paradiesli…»

Diese kleine Begebenheit – ausgewählt aus Dutzend von ähnlichen Erlebnissen – deutet die spezielle Beziehung zwischen uns an. Durch unzählige gemeinsame Erlebnisse, beruflich und privat, hat sich eine tiefe Freundschaft entwickelt. Die Begegnung hat mich nicht nur privat und seelisch bereichert, sondern auch beruflich bin ich weitergekommen: Durch ständige Fotositzungen habe ich meinen Stil als Zauberer weiterentwickelt und vieles überhaupt erst verstanden. Dies ist eine der ganz grossen Fähigkeiten von Christoph: Beim Fotographieren geht er auf die Person ein, versucht, die Hintergründe, Emotionen, Schwächen und Stärken zu spüren und all dies ins Bild einzubringen. Ja, Christoph, mein lieber Freund, wenn man bei Dir Modell steht, ist das keine passive Rolle. Mit jeder Minute lernt man sich besser kennen, spürt neue Dimensionen, ahnt noch Unentdecktes. Dafür möchte ich Dir an dieser Stelle meinen herzlichen Dank aussprechen! Tage, Abende und Nächte hängen wir zusammen herum, gehen essen, ins Kino, Theater, Konzert. Gegenseitig jammern wir uns die Ohren voll über finanzielle Probleme, Ärger im Beruf, Misserfolge bei Frauen (wobei das letzte klar überwiegt). Und was gibt es Schöneres als einen Leidgenossen! Ah ja, was seine fotografischen Arbeiten angeht: Nun, ich als Laie wage da kein Urteil abzugeben. Ich weiss nur eines: sein Stil in der Fotografie gefällt mir. Bilder von ihm kann ich immer wieder betrachten, immer wieder finde ich neue sehenswerte Details. Nehmen Sie sich die Zeit, dieses Buch, diese herrlichen Bilder anzusehen, auf sich wirken zu lassen. Sie werden sehen, was ich meine.

Christoph Borer

Lilian Esther Krauthammer-Perrin. Geboren 1965 in Bern. Trotz intensiver Zeichenversuche als Kind stand der Berufswunsch Medizin bald im Vordergrund. Doch kurz vor Abschluss brach sie das Gymnasium ab, um das Vorjahr der Kunstgewerbeschule in Bern zu besuchen. Die Faszination zur Grafik bewog Lilian Krauthammer, während vier Jahren dieses Handwerk zu erlernen. Bereits während der obligatorischen Praktika war für sie eines klar: sie wollte von Anfang an selbständig arbeiten. 1985 Eröffnung des eigenen Ateliers mit ersten Aufträgen, trotz Warnungen von allen Seiten, 1986 Abschlussprüfung. Im gleichen Jahr erhielt sie das Eidgenössische Stipendium für angewandte Kunst. Ihre Abschlussarbeit war gleichzeitig die Gestaltung ihres ersten Buches, das sie für die Dissertation eines Arztes gestaltet hat: «Wir haben ein Asthmakind», Kösel Verlag München. Seit kurzem ist Lilian Krauthammer mit ihrem Atelier nach Zürich gezogen.

Christoph Grünig. Born in Berne in 1958 and brought up in Berne and Bienne. After serving his apprenticeship as a photographer in Thun he worked as a freelance for two years with established photographers. In 1982 he decided to set up on his own and opened an advertising photography studio in Bienne. His guiding principle, "People at centre stage", is just as constant a companion as his camera, and he remains true to it not only in hotels but in the Provence and Andalusia, where he lives for part of the time.

The photographs in this book were taken with a Nikon F4 (he had first tried a small, discreet camera, to which the hotel "inmates" did not react at all); the focal lengths were from 20 to 35 and 105 millimetres. The films used were Kodak T-Max 400 and 3200.

Christoph on Christoph

I'm walking home. "I could really go out and have a meal with Stöh today… hm… perhaps in the Paradiesli again." When I get home, a call is waiting for me on the answerer: "Hello, this is Stöh. We could have a meal out again, couldn't we? I'd suggest the Paradiesli…"

This little episode—chosen from dozens of similar incidents—gives a hint of our special relationship. A deep friendship has developed between us, fed by innumerable shared experiences in our business and private lives. Meeting Stöh has not been only a spiritual enrichment for me, I have profited in my profession too. As a result of our constant photographic sessions I have developed my style as a magician and have come to understand a lot of things I hadn't realized before. This is one of Christoph's outstanding abilities: in his photographs he occupies himself with the person before him, tries to sense the background qualities, the emotions, the strengths and weaknesses, and to capture these in his pictures. Yes, Christoph, my dear friend, sitting for you is no passive part. One gets to know oneself better every minute, one is aware of new dimensions, makes new discoveries. I'd like to take this opportunity to convey my heartfelt thanks! We move around together for days, evenings, nights at a time, go for dinner, to the cinema, the theatre or a concert together. We moan endlessly about our financial problems, worries at work, disappointments with women (especially this last item). What else is as comforting as a companion in misfortune! As for his photographs, as a layman I can't presume to pass a critical judgement. I only know that I like his photographic style. I can look at his pictures again and again, and I always find new and worthwhile details in them. Just take your time to study this book, these splendid shots, and to let them sink in. You'll see exactly what I mean.

Christoph Borer

Lilian Esther Krauthammer-Perrin. Born in Berne in 1965. Although she busily exercised her drawing skills as a child, when she had to choose a profession she opted for medicine. But shortly before completing her high-school studies, she left to attend the preparatory year in the Arts and Crafts School in Berne. The fascination of graphic art was so strong that she spent four years studying it. One thing was clear to her even during the obligatory practical training periods: she wanted to work on her own account from the outset. In 1985 she opened her own studio after obtaining her first assignments, although warnings came from all sides. In 1986 she took her final examination. In the same year she won a Swiss federal scholarship for applied art. Her leaving exercise was her first book design, intended for a doctor's thesis: "Wir haben ein Asthmakind", published by Kösel, Munich. Lilian Krauthammer recently moved to a new studio in Zurich.